The
Know- Nothing
Party.

A Sketch
By Humphrey J. Desmond.

Washington:
The New Century Press.
1905

PREFACE.

A GENERAL view of the Nativist Movement in American politics has many points of interest for the student of history, and not a few instructive lessons probably applicable to future conditions. Movements of this nature are quite likely to recur; if, perhaps, in a somewhat varied and feebler form, nevertheless in their salient characteristics, closely modeled after the Know-Nothing party of 1854.

In the pages of Von Holst and Rhodes, in the special pleadings of Lee and Whitney, in more careful local studies such as those of Scisco, in the annals of Congress, in the biographies or memoirs of men prominent in American public life fifty years ago, in the political text books of the time, and in a variety of other publications, there is a vast amount of information bearing upon the Nativist and Know-Nothing movements; but, so far as the writer of these pages is able to ascertain, no attempt has heretofore been made to gather, from all the best sources, a survey at once complete (at least within the limitations of brevity here proposed), connected and free from the spirit of advocacy.

CONTENTS.

NATIVE-AMERICANISM.

THE KNOW-NOTHING PARTY.

Native Americanism.

I.

A PRELIMINARY VIEW.

LOOKING back, from the threshold of a new century, at the movements of Nativism and anti-Catholicism which transpired in the United States during the period 1835-60, we can feel little surprise in the premises. The mighty immigrations of the nineteenth century jostled the settled colonists of the seventeenth and eighteenth centuries, established here in a political and industrial ascendancy. A total of over five million immigrants landed on our shores up to 1850; a total of nearly twenty million up to 1900. At the close of the century over ten million foreign born persons are residents of the United States, and more than twenty-six million* of the sixty-six million white inhabitants are of foreign parentage; making it quite certain that a majority of the Americans of today are descendants of forefathers who came here since Jefferson was president—the old Americans of Revolutionary lineage being outnumbered by the children of ancestors who were not here when Washington lived.

So mighty an invasion, peaceable though it was, could not transpire without much collision and many readjustments. The arrival in our large cities of thousands of immigrants, differing in race and religion from the native inhabitants, created conditions for social and political compromise. The Irish, for instance, while exhibiting a capacity to assimilate their neighbors, and sometimes (as in the case of the Norman and English settlers in Ireland) to make them "more

* By the census of 1900 more than half the people of foreign parentage in this country are of non-English speaking races. More than half, too, are in race neither Teutonic nor Anglo-Saxon.

8

Irish than the Irish themselves"—also have, for some reason or other, excited antagonisms more bitter than assailed any other race of immigrants.†

In the sequel, Nativism met with utter defeat in all its cherished contentions; yet substantially the victory was on the side of the Americans of the older lineage. There was always a larger-viewed element among them disposed to welcome immigration to this country as "the asylum of the oppressed;" to see in the imported brawn of the Irish and German, material for national enrichment—the industrial army needed for the develop-

---

† Scisco, in his "History of Political Nativism in New York," says (ch. I.): "An anonymous writer to the press touched on the truth when he complained of the Irish Catholics that 'they are men, who having professed to become Americans by accepting our terms of naturalization, do yet, in direct contradiction to their professions, clan together as a separate interest and retain their foreign appellation.' No better statement of Nativist complaint could have been made." Yet to a large extent this going apart of the Irish was but natural, in view of the contemptuous manner in which the "nativist" Americans treated them, ridiculing their appearance, their country and their religion.

9

ment of the country. History, too, records no more notable instance of speedy and complete assimilation of a vast influx of population. The social, political and educational institutions of the Americans of Revolutionary lineage survived and absorbed and won over the mighty army of immigrants, and welded all elements into a unified nationality.

There never was any deep-seated antipathy to foreigners, as such, in this country. Nativism in its restricted sense (dislike of European immigrants on account of their birth) was always more or less accidental and sporadic. It is usual in discussing the genesis of the Native-American movement to refer to the Alien acts of 1798 as one of the first manifestations of this feeling, or to the mythical order of Washington at Valley Forge: "Put none but Americans on guard tonight."

That which gave Native-Americanism its real strength and animus, however, was anti-Catholicism;‡ and

‡ Brownson in his Quarterly Review for January 1845, in a survey of Native Americanism, says that the real objection to the

the roots of this feeling lie far back in colonial days. The colonists carried the "No Popery" sentiment from their English homes. Founded on sectarian lines, the colonies naturally were more deeply tinctured with this feeling than was England herself; and circumstances, such as warfare with the French Catholics on the north and west, and with the Spanish Catholics in Florida, deepened the sentiment. One reason that the French-Canadians did not join with the American colonies in revolt against England was their sense of being fairly treated, by the English, in their religious interests; and although the continental congress sent a Catholic priest§ among its emissaries to them, with proffers of an equal partnership and independent statehood, they distrusted colonial bigotry. France's providential assistance to the struggling colonies, the presence of her Catholic soldiers with their af-

foreigner lay deeper than the accident of birth. "The party is truly an anti-Catholic party."

§ This was Rev. John Carroll afterwards the first Catholic bishop of the United States.

fable chaplains and courteous officers, remained a liberalizing memory with the Revolutionary generation.

From 1780 to 1830—a period of fifty years—the No Popery sentiment slept with but little awakening. The brief crusade against aliens during the latter part of Adams' administration was strictly incidental to the division between the parties—the Jeffersonian party, as the friend of France, having the adhesion naturally of all the French, Irish and Scotch immigrants of that time. The Alien act which had extended the period of residence required for naturalization to fourteen years, was repealed in 1802, and the five years' requirement of residence restored. The demand made by the Hartford Convention (1814-15), that aliens be debarred from civil office‖ may have been suggested by the enthusiasm with which the Irish immigrants hailed the war of 1812—so unpopular with New England. British Minister Foster, who had labored to prevent this war, said that among the

‖ This was one of the seven amendments to the constitution proposed by the Hartford Convention.

congressmen who voted to declare war were six members of the Society of United Irishmen.**

There was really little ground for alarm in the number of immigrants which reached our shores in the decades ending with 1840. Up to 1820 foreigners came to America at the rate of 10,000 a year. From 1821 to 1830, inclusive, 143,439 landed. From 1831 to 1840, the immigration increased to a total of nearly 600,000, or about three per cent. of the total population (seventeen millions) in 1840. From 1840-50 (principally in the last half of the decade) 1,700,000 immigrants arrived, or seven per cent. of the population in 1850. The percentage of the foreign born population in the decades prior to 1850 was considerably less than it has been since the close of the Civil War. In 1850 the foreign born element was 9.7 per cent. of the whole population. During the period 1860-1900 it has varied between 13 and 14 per cent.

The really alarming symptom was

** See Alexander Johnston's article on "The American Party," in the "American Cyclopaedia of Politics."

tLe large proportion of Catholics among the immigrants. More than a third of the immigrants for the decades ending 1830 and 1840 were from Ireland, and nearly one-half of the 1,700,000 who landed from 1841-50 were Irish. More than a half, and probably nearly three-fifths, of the immigrants up to 1860 were Catholics.

It is probable that the English "No-Popery" agitation (1815-29), which antagonized the movement for Catholic emancipation in Ireland and England, had some influence in alarming the more sectarian portion of the American public. The opposition to Catholic emancipation in England necessarily reverted to the position of Elizabeth's and Cromwell's time—that the Catholic religion was not entitled to toleration—that it was a political danger—that it inculcated a divided allegiance, etc. This argument was adopted in America. The pulpit alarmist could point to new object lessons, up to this time unfamiliar to the American population: bishops (there were only ten American Catholic bishops in 1833), cathedrals (rather unpre-

14

tentious affairs), sisterhoods in a peculiar garb and convents or nunneries.

A consciousness of this change in public feeling is shown in some passages which occur in the pastoral issued in 1833 by the Catholic bishops on the occasion of their second provincial council. They refer to the calumnies current in the press. "We notice with regret," they say, "a spirit exhibited by some of the conductors of the press engaged in the interest of those brethren separated from our communion, which has, within a few years, been more unkind and unjust in our regard. Not only do they assail us and our institutions in a style of vituperation and offence. * * but they have even denounced you as enemies of the republic, etc."

The first outbreak of nativism occurred in 1834—the burning of the Ursuline convent at Charlestown, near Boston. In 1833, one Rebecca Reed had left this institution and told such tales of harsh treatment that when, in the following year, Miss Harrison (Sister Mary John), left the same convent in a dazed and hysterical condition, the public became excited. She

15

suffered from nervous prostration caused by overwork in preparing her pupils for an exhibition. Her brother induced her to return to the convent, where she was placed under a physician's care. On August 9, 1834, a mob composed of the lower element of Boston's population, surrounded the the convent, and, although Miss Harrison came forth and assured them that she was not detained against her will, they ransacked and burned the building. The better class of Boston citizens held an indignation meeting in Fanueil hall, at which the mayor presided, and the outrage was denounced. The perpetrators were put on trial, but weakly prosecuted and consequently acquitted. The sisters never obtained compensation for their loss of property, although a committee of the Legislature subsequently recommended this act of public justice.

In 1836 a book was published which has been termed "The Uncle Tom's Cabin of Know-Nothingism. Maria Monk, a girl of evil character, had been placed by her mother in a Magdalen asylum at Montreal, under the charge of a Catholic sisterhood. Aided by a former paramour, she escaped and shortly fell into the company of one Rev. J. J. Slocum, who, with others, concocted a sensational and obscene narrative of her experience in the assumed capacity of a nun. This book was brought out with Howe & Bates as nominal publishers—these men being employees of Harper Brothers (which publishing firm, it is said, really stood behind the enterprise, but was reluctant to assume direct responsibility). Maria Monk's "disclosures" had an immense sale, exceeding that of any American book up to that time published. Ministers recommended it and churches feted its author. She was taken into the bosom of Christian homes, where, after a time, her depravity was perceived. It is to be regretted that one so useful to evangelicalism should have been allowed to sink in the social scale so that she afterwards died in a public institution. The parties to this literary enterprise began litigation among themselves for the profits. A party of Protestant clergymen visited Montreal to verify the "awful disclosures" and pronounced them a fabrication. Colonel W. L. Stone, editor of The New York Commercial Advertiser, also made a thorough investigation, visiting the Hotel Dieu at Montreal from cellar to garret. "The result," he wrote, "is the most thorough conviction that Maria Monk is an arrant impostor, that she never was a nun, etc."

These two early manifestations of anti-Catholicism are particularly dwelt upon because they are prototypes of its campaign tactics in the following years. Edward Wilson, in 1845, Gavazzi and the "Angel Gabriel" in 1853-5, and a score of others followed in the line of Maria Monk; and what Professor John B. McMaster calls the "riotous career of Know-Nothings," was a repetition of the convent burning of 1834. The ex-priest, the escaped nun and the incendiary led the way, as the radical exponents of a cause, which nevertheless numbered among its followers some respectable elements.

In the year following 1830, a new exuberance overtook the electoral life of the American people. They talked politics with vigor and gesticulation; they interrupted each others political meetings; they jostled each other at the polls. It became part of the election day program for each party to be represented at the voting precincts by partisans, loud of lungs and strong of arm. The native American had practiced all the tricks and frauds of politics, such as intimidating voters, stuffing ballot boxes, repeating and tampering with the returns, long before the foreigner was instructed in these processes. In the history of the Abolition movement, we have an illustration of the riotous spirit of the American politics of that generation. In 1835, Thompson, an Abolition advocate, was mobbed in Boston and forced to leave the city. Garrison, too, felt the wrath of "a broadcloth mob." November 7, 1837, Lovejoy, an Abolitionist editor, was murdered at Alton, Ill., because he refused to suspend his publication. May 17, 1838, Pennsylvania hall, the Abolitionist headquarters at Philadelphia, was burned to the ground by the intolerant opponents of the anti-slavery movement. And thus on to 1860, did Abolitionism meet with disorderly and riotous opposition. The party factions quarrelled with each other, Whigs assailed Whigs, and Democrats assailed Democrats. The expression "Loco Focos" applied to one of the Democratic factions in New York, originated over the incident of an interrupted meeting (October 29, 1835). Emissaries of one Democratic faction turned off the lights at a meeting held by another faction. Immediately the engloomed Democrats, who had prepared for the emergency beforehand, took from their pockets the new Loco Foco match which had just come into use, and relighted their meeting.

Know-Nothingism ran its course at a time when this sort of exuberant politics had reached its climax. The Know-Nothings were not the inventors, but they carried the method, especially in Baltimore, to its worst excesses.*

From a survey of disorder of this kind, we are led to wonder where the

* Volunteer fire companies, which existed in the principal cities of the United States at this time, were largely responsible for street disorders. There was an intense rivalry between the companies, and sometimes fires were started on purpose to bring the rival firemen into collision.

American notion of free speech developed; yet it did evolve. If at first a mere glittering generality; if more honored in the breach than in the observance; if more as a pretence than a practice, it was nevertheless finally fixed in the customs and principles of the people.

II.

NATIVISM IN LOCAL POLITICS.

THE first political flurry of Nativism in the local politics of New York seems to date from the year 1835. It is associated with the name of Samuel F. B. Morse, the inventor of the telegraph. Early in 1834 he published twelve letters in The New York Observer (a weekly paper), over the signature of "Brutus." These were afterwards republished under the title "Foreign Conspiracy Against the United States," a book much read up to 1860.

It appears that while in Europe during 1829-32, Morse had heard of the Leopold Foundation, an Aid Society established in Austria to help with financial assistance the missionary and poor

NATIVE AMERICANISM.

Catholic churches of the New World. This was the most material fact in the dangers Morse discussed. The "Brutus Letters" had an important local influence. The Irish immigrants in the city were gathering antagonisms, chiefly on account of their religion, and the "Brutus Letters" gave form to the argument. A Protestant association was founded to antagonize the Catholics, and it seems that on March 13, 1835, one of its meetings on Broadway was disturbed by Irish interruption, perhaps after the fashion common at that time of counter demonstrations at public meetings; but rather imprudent tactics for foreigners.

In the fall election a Nativist committee put up Colonel Monroe (a nephew of ex-President Monroe), for Congress, and the Whigs endorsed him. But the Democrats, who cast three-fifths of the vote, elected their ticket. In the spring election of 1836, the Nativists nominated Samuel F. B. Morse for mayor, and he received about 1,-500 votes out of a total of over 26,-000 cast. A Democratic mayor was elected. The Nativists tried a separate ticket again in the fall elections, with no better success; but in the spring of 1837 they put up Aaron Clark for mayor, and at the same time drew up an address denouncing the Irish. The Whig party,† which had all along exhibited a kindly interest in the Nativist doings, endorsed Clark, and he was elected by 3,300 plurality. The affair was treated as a Whig victory, and the Nativists disappeared as a separate political activity. Nativist sentiment continued, however, to exhibit itself in petitions to the state legislature and to Congress, praying for a registry law and an extension of the period of residence required for naturalization to twenty-one years.

In other portions of the country the same sentiment manifested itself. A native American movement is said to have organized at Germantown, near Philadelphia, in 1837, growing out of

† In New York city the Irish vote was cast largely with the Democratic party. Admiration for Andrew Jackson, the hero of New Orleans and a man of Irish lineage, had drawn the vanguards of Irish immigration close in sympathy with the Democratic party. The politicians of that party did not fail to use every means to attach the adopted citizen to their organization.

an election episode.

At Boston on Sunday, June 11, 1837, an engine company returning from a fire came into collision with an Irish funeral procession. The ensuing trouble, which is known in the annals of Boston as "the Broad street riot," was participated in by fifteen thousand persons. The Irish quarter was sacked, and though there were no fatalities, many persons were severely wounded. The intervention of the mayor at the head of a military company quelled the riot. As a result of this affair, the fire department was reorganized (Winsor's Boston III, 245).

Boston had a Nativist mayor, Thomas Aspinwall Davis, in 1845, as a result of a triangular contest. In the following year the control of the city reverted to the Whigs.

During the presidential campaign of 1840, the Whig central committee of Maryland was moved to formally repudiate all sympathy with the Nativist journalism of General Duff Green, editor of The Baltimore Pilot. The committee declared that "the native and natural citizens are equally entitled to the blessings of our government." Maryland was, politically, a close state. The Whigs carried the state at the ensuing election. Similar action was taken by a large Whig public meeting at Louisville, Ky. (October 27, 1840). Its resolutions recited that "a newspaper called The Louisville Tribune, reflecting on the Catholic persuasion, of a most anti-republican character, recently established in this city, professing to be a Whig paper, has published editorials and a communication, one of which is signed 'Native American,' etc. The Whigs as a party, therefore, utterly repudiate and denounce The Louisville Tribune." (McClusky Political Text Book, pp. 681-2.)

New Orleans felt the impulse also. The "Address of the Louisiana Native American association," issued in 1839, contains this rather ornate passage:

"So long as foreigners entered in moderate numbers into the states and territories of the United States and became imperceptibly merged and incorporated into the great body of the American people, and were gradually imbued and indoctrinated into the principles of virtue and patriotism, which formerly animated the whole

26

American community, so long their advent was an advantage and a benefit to our community. But when we see hordes and hecatombs (sic) of beings in human forms, but destitute of any intellectual aspirations—the outcast and offal of society, the pauper, the vagrant and the convict—transported in myriads to our shores, reeking with the accumulated crimes of the whole civilized and savage world, and inducted by our laws into equal rights, immunities and privileges with the noble native inhabitants of the United States, we can no longer contemplate it with supine indifference. We feel constrained to warn our countrymen that unless some steps are taken to protect our institutions from these accumulated inroads on our national character, from the indiscriminate immigration and naturalization of foreigners, in vain have our predecessors, whether native or naturalized, toiled and suffered and fought and bled and died to achieve our liberties and establish our hallowed institutions."

In 1841, a state convention was called in Louisiana to form an American Republican party. The convention favored the exclusion of foreigners from office. It exerted some influence in the succeeding municipal election in New Orleans.‖

New York city, in 1840, had a population of 312,700, of whom not over a third were foreign born. The Catholic population of the city possessed eight churches and numbered perhaps 70,000. Philadelphia, in the same year, had a population of 258,000, of whom less than sixty thousand were Catholics. (Bishop Kenrick, in 1840, placed the entire Catholic population of Pennsylvania, Delaware and Western New Jersey at 120,000.) Boston, with a population in 1844 of about 120,000, had less than 30,000 Catholic residents. It seemed strange, in view of what has come to pass in later years, that the presence in these larger cities of a foreign population not exceeding a fourth of the whole population, should have occasioned alarm in the

‖ Congressman Eustis, of Louisiana, in the House of Representatives, January 7, 1856, claimed that Louisiana was the first State whose Legislature called for an extension of the term of residence required for naturalization.

minds of Americans during the '40's. Since these days, the increased tide of immigration has foreignized, by actual majorities (counting all of foreign parentage), most of our large cities and even some of our western states, without the slightest danger to our institutions or any similar alarm to our people.

Had the foreigners and Catholics remained quiescent, Nativism might have run its course as a milder protest. But this was not to be. The American atmosphere would not suffer any element long to demean itself as a subject class. The colonization of the nineteenth century challenged, in the name of religious equality, the Protestant ascendancy established by the colonists of the seventeenth century in the laws, and customs, and opinions of the several states. In Massachusetts, long after the adoption of the Federal constitution, Congregationalism was virtually the religion of the state. In the Carolinas a Catholic could not hold office. Other states, like New Hampshire, had similar sectarian provisions in their constitutions and statutes.

Immigration endangered this ascen-

29

dancy, and as soon as that fact was apparent, the Protestant pulpit became alarmed. The particular issue in which this clash of forces came had reference to the schools. Under the New York school law of 1812, denominational schools received a pro rata share of the school fund raised by the state. But in New York city a private corporation called the Public School society, gradually absorbed all the public funds for that city. It claimed to be an unsectarian body, and declared that it excluded positive religious instruction from its schools. The Protestant Scriptures, however, were read, and in some cases commented upon. The Catholics presented a petition to the Common council, and Bishop Hughes spoke in its behalf, praying that eight Catholic schools be granted a share of the school fund (October, 1840). The Catholics do not appear to have asked the exclusion of the Bible, but prejudice was stirred upon the representation that such was their purpose.

The Common council, which was Democratic, rejected the bishop's petition after a full hearing, in which the

Public School society fought strenuously for its monopoly. The Catholics thereupon carried their grievances to the state Legislature at Albany. William H. Seward was then governor of New York. He had expressed himself in favor of the establishment of schools where the foreigners, now debarred from public education by religious prejudices, might be instructed by teachers of their own race and faith. For twenty years (1840-60) this idea of Seward's made him the target of the political anti-Catholics in New York state, and he reciprocated that antagonism by holding the major element of the Whig party intact as a bulwark against the successive waves of Nativist and Know-Nothing assimilation.*

The Catholic appeal to the Legisla-

* Colonel A. K. McClure, in his "Political Recollections," asserts that Seward's attitude on the school question lost him the nomination to the Presidency in 1860; that the leaders of the Republican party in Pennsylvania, Ohio and Indiana were favorable to Seward personally, but on account of his stand in the New York school controversy they could not hope to attract to his candidacy the anti-slavery Know-Nothing vote in those states, which were regarded at the time as doubtful states.

ture again stirred up a Nativist party, Samuel F. B. Morse once more occupying the leadership. All local parties having taken sides with the Public School society in the nomination of candidates for the Legislature in 1841, Bishop Hughes decided to put up a Catholic ticket—the so-called "Carroll Hall" ticket. He did this against the vociferous objections of the entire local press, Democratic as well as Whig. The resultt of the election was as follows:

Whig ticket..	15,980
Democratic ticket..	15,690
Catholic ticket..	2,200
Nativist ticket..	470
Anti-Slavery ticket..	120

It was said that Bishop Hughes (himself, if anything, a Whig), had sought to show to the Democrats that the Catholics held the balance of power in New York city as between the Whig and the Democratic parties. He succeeded in the demonstration, at least to the extent of defeating the Democratic ticket, which would otherwise have won. But it seems that only a half or a third of the Catholic

‡ See New York Tribune, Nov. 12, 1841.

voters supported the Carroll Hall ticket. In a Catholic population of 70,-000, there were at that time probably from 5,000 to 7,000 Catholic voters in New York city.‖

The following year the Legislature at Albany, doubtless through the influence of Governor Seward, extended to New York city the provisions of the general act relating to common schools. thus obliterating the private Public School society corporation, and putting the state and the people in its place as a controlling power over the city schools. This was a victory, in principle, for Bishop Hughes, but it brought no funds to his parish schools. The Nativist element of all parties combined for some years in electing a union school ticket.

‖ This is the only instance in American politics of a Catholic ticket at the polls. It seemed necessary at the time to clear the political atmosphere. Of course it did not lack provocation either, in the existence of a menacing anti-Catholic movement.

III.

NATIVISM AT HIGH TIDE, 1844.

THE year 1843 saw a new and better organized spurt of Nativism in New York city. The episode that served to arouse it was the favor shown by the Democratic party to the Irish, in return for Irish support in the April (1843) elections. Not only were petty offices liberally bestowed, but market licenses were given to foreign-born tradesmen. Heretofore these had been (as in the case of school control), a species of Nativist monopoly.

The American Republican party was formed,§ and it came into the fall elec-

§ The following appears among the declarations of the Nativist meeting held in New York, June 10, 1843:

"Resolved, That we as Americans will

34

tions with a statement of principles, among which was the following:

"That through this school law [the legislative enactment of April, 1842] there has been a preconcerted determination, followed up by an actual attempt in the Fourth ward, to put out of our schools the Protestant Bible, and to put down the whole Protestant religion

never consent to allow the government established by our Revolutionary forefathers to pass into the hands of foreigners, and that while we open the door to the oppressed of every nation and offer a home and an asylum, we reserve to ourselves the right of administering the government in conformity with the principles laid down by those who have committed it to our care."

From this time on we hear much about the degeneracy of American local politics, due, so it is alleged, to the influence of the foreign-born voters. There has always been a strong suspicion that this opinion was merely the result of Nativist prejudice. Bryce (Volume II. of his "American Commonwealth," page 241), says: "Nevertheless the immigrants are not so largely responsible for the faults of American politics as a stranger might be led, by the language of many Americans, to suppose. There is a disposition in the United States to use them, and especially the Irish, much as the cat is used in the kitchen, to account for broken plates and food which disappears. The cities have, no doubt, suffered from the immigrants—but New York was not an Eden before the Irish came."

[therein] as being sectarian." (Journal of Commerce, November 4, 1843.)

The platform further demanded that foreign-born persons should not be naturalized until they had resided here twenty-one years. The Nativist party polled 8,690 votes in the November election out of a total of 37,000. Its strength appears to have been drawn quite equally from both parties. Hammond, in his "Political History of New York," avers that "the wealth, talent and respectability of the community" went into its ranks. In the ensuing election (April, 1844), the Nativist party selected James Harper, of the firm of Harper Brothers, publishers, as its candidate for mayor. Both Democrats and Whigs made their customary nominations; but there was a tacit understanding among the Whigs that their support should be thrown largely to Harper (who had been a Whig). Harper was electel. The vote stood: Harper, 24,510; Coddington (Dem.), 20,538; Franklin (Whig), 5,297. The Journal of Commerce (April 12, 1884), estimated that the native American vote was made up of 14,100 Whigs, 9,700 Democrats and 601 new voters.

NATIVE AMERICANISM.

Harper's election was the occasion
for a revival of the former alliance between the Whigs and the Nativist. In
the fall election of 1844 (which was also a presidential election), the Whigs
threw their strength solidly to the Nativist local legislative ticket, but the
Nativists did not fully reciprocate.
The Nativist legislative ticket was
elected, 27,440 to 26,230 (Dem.), but
Polk, the Democratic candidate for
president, carried New York city by
several thousand plurality over Clay.
Seward had openly disapproved of the
Whig alliance with the Nativists, and
this experience strengthened the position he had taken. The Whigs proceeded
to drop the Nativists. At the city election in April, 1845, Harper was defeated and a Democratic mayor elected,
the poll showing 24,210 Democratic
votes, 17,480 Nativist and 7,030 Whig.
The Nativists were almost completely
wiped off the official roster, electing
but one of their candidates, a consta-
ble. They continued to put up local
tickets until April, 1847, but their
vote diminished from 8,370 in November, 1845, to 2,080 in April, 1847.
They put up a state ticket in 1846,

which received an aggregate of 6,170 votes.

Bishop Hughes in an editorial published February 3, 1844, in a weekly paper, The Freeman's Journal, regarded as the organ of the diocese, had alluded to the new party as a movement in "local politics." "Many will probably join this party, who are really friends of foreigners," he said, " but who, for the moment, will coalesce with their enemies to accomplish some local purpose, of which foreigners form no part. The true issue is for the loaves and fishes of office, and as but a small share of these, if any, falls to the lot of foreigners, so, notwithstanding the abuse of their name, they may consider themselves as scarcely interested in the quarrel. The true issue is between natives and natives; there let it remain."

The school question was also one of the mainsprings of the Nativist movement in Philadelphia. In this connection it may be remarked that in the many subsequent clashes with Protestant ascendancy, of which the New York and Philadelphia instances were among the earliest, the Catholic contention was, ultimately, almost everywhere successful, because it was grounded on the logic of religious equality.

If the Maine supreme court in 1854 (Donohue vs. Richards) decided that Catholic pupils in the public schools might be compelled to read the King James Bible, the victory of sectarianism was only temporary; the decision of the Wisconsin supreme court in 1890 (Edgerton Bible case) brought to a climax a series of educational rulings, both in law and practice, which have quite generally excluded the Bible from the public schools and more or less eliminated the offensive tone to Catholics of many of the text books, against which there were mild protests in 1840.

In November, 1842, Bishop Kenrick of Philadelphia, while not asking that the Bible be excluded from the public schools of that city, petitioned the School Board that Catholic children be allowed the liberty of using the Catholic version where Bible reading was prescribed.

In January, 1843, the Philadelphia School Board voted that no children whose parents objected to Bible reading be obliged to be present at Bible exercises. Out of this matter a controversy ensued, and Bishop Kenrick, on March 12, 1844, issued a statement that "Catholics have not asked that the Bible be excluded from the public schools."

The Philadelphia riots of May, 1844, are connected with this episode, at least in the opinion of the grand jury called to investigate the affair. The grand jury attributed the riots to "the efforts of a portion of the community to exclude the Bible from the public school." The Catholics denied this and claimed the jury was packed. But the charge, even as it stands, would not in our day seem to justify or provoke rioting or incendiarism. The disorder arose over some collision in the streets as a Native-American meeting was dispersing before a rain storm. The riots which followed lasted for three days. Though the Mayor was knocked down in one of the encounters, it is probably true, as the Catholics alleged, that there was half-heartedness, if not actual collusion, in the way the authorities met the disorder. The mob moved upon the Irish quarter in Kensington and burned twenty-nine houses. Next day two Catholic churches, St. Michael's and St. Augustine's, were destroyed and a convent set ablaze. A number of lives were lost. Bishop Kenrick issued a card suspending "the exercise of public worship in the Catholic churches which still remained until it can be resumed with safety and we can enjoy our constitutional rights to worship God according to the dictates of our conscience."

This was, at least, furnishing subject of meditation for the thoughtful. The May riots were succeeded in July by another riotous outbreak. The Nativist sentiment profited by the public feeling against the foreigners, which had been aroused by the events of May. Their societies were now established in every ward of the city. On July 4, 1844, they organized an elaborate parade in which 4,500 men and boys participated. During the succeeding days a report became current that arms were hidden in St. Philip Neri's (Catholic) church. There was foundation for this report too. Catholics had feared that the church burning of May might be repeated. They intended to defend their property. The collision of July was principally between the militia and the nativist mobs. It resulted in seventeen deaths.

Nativism remained for some years a political power in Philadelphia. The local leader of the party was Lewis C. Levin, by birth a South Carolinian, a man of stout build and florid eloquence. For three terms he sat as a representative of the first Pennsylvania district in Congress where he made many impassioned anti-Catholic speeches. Levin died in 1860. Throughout the country generally, however, the Philadelphia riots gave Nativism a set back. The popular verdict blamed the anti-Catholics. General Cadwalader, who had commanded the soldiers during the riots, some years afterwards stated in a public letter that the Nativists came to be generally known as the "the church burners," in the epithet parlance of the day.*

*Scisco, "Political Nativism in New York," page 47, says: "The Philadelphia riots, nevertheless, lost much sympathy to

In New York, Bishop Hughes, admonished by these events, took legal advice as to whether compensation could be obtained for property destroyed by rioters. Being advised in the negative, he said: "Then the law intends that citizens should defend their own property." He issued an extra edition of The Freeman's Journal, calling on Catholics to defend their churches with their lives. The Native-Americans, who had called a public meeting, revoked their call in view of this action. Bishop O'Gorman ("History Catholic Church," p. 375) tells us that a large Irish society in New York, with divisions in every district, resolved that, in case a single Catholic church were destroyed, to fire buildings in all quarters and involve the city in a great conflagration.

Though the field of its action was mostly confined to local politics, the Native-American movement had some results in the broader arena (1830-45).

While most of the foreign-born vote was Democratic, the Whigs were not

the cause of Nativism, and their occurrence was deeply regretted."

without a share of it. Bishop Hughes, for instance, tells us that his first vote was cast for Henry Clay. In the campaign of 1840, the Democratic leaders of New York corralled almost the solid naturalized vote by representing that Harrison was opposed to the "adopted citizen." This provoked Whig resentment. "Do we not hear of the organization of a party against the Catholics?" wrote Seward to a friend in 1840. Some of the Whig leaders, like Clay, Scott and Fillmore, undoubtedly sympathized with the principles of the Native-American party. In 1844 Clay wrote to a friend: "There is a general tendency among the Whigs to unfurl the banner of the Native-American party" (Von Holst II., 524). Scott in The National Intelligencer (December, 1844), advocated the practical exclusion of all foreign-born persons from the suffrage.† Later he claimed that the Mexican war had removed the cataract from his eyes. (Von Holst, IV.,

---

†Brownson in his Quarterly Review for January, 1845, refers disparagingly to a speech by Webster at Faneuil hall, in which he thinks that this man of "transcendant abilities" pandered to the Nativist feeling.

158).

New York was a pivotal state in the Presidential election held in November, 1844. Polk polled just 5,106 more votes in New York than Clay, and this gave him New York's thirty-six electoral votes, and the Presidency. Millard Fillmore, in a letter to Clay, attributed the loss of New York to Catholic defection from the Whigs, occasioned by the affiliation of Native-Americanism with that party. Anti-Masonry had deprived Clay of the Presidential nomination in 1840, and between Native-Americanism and the Liberal party he lost the election in 1844. But the resentment of the naturalized voters was not all due, properly, to the Whigs. The aid of a fair percentage of the Democratic party always went to the proscriptive ticket. In the fall election of 1844 this Democratic contingent, while voting generally for the Polk electors, in Philadelphia and New York enabled the Native-Americans to elect their local tickets.

In April, 1845, the Nativist movement claimed 48,000 members in New York State (of whom 18,000 were in New York city), 42,000 in Pennsylvania, 14,000 in Massachusetts and 6,000 scattered in other states. (Rochester American, April 26, 1845). A convention of the Native-Americans convened at Philadelphia July 4, 1845, with 141 delegates present, representing fourteen states. It adopted a national platform and an address to the people. A second national convention met May 4, 1847, at Pittsburg, with eleven states represented. At its second session at Philadelphia, September 10, 1847, it recommended Zachary Taylor for President.

Six Native-American Congressmen, (four from New York and two from Pennsylvania) were elected to the Twenty-ninth Congress (1845). But one Native-American Congressman appeared in the Thirtieth Congress and none in the Thirty-first.

The Mexican war had come and gone (1846-8). A great event had set new currents afloat. Native-Americanism began to disappear. Both parties were again courting the naturalized citizen whom the Irish famine was sending to our shores in vaster numbers. Candidates were found purging themselves from the suspicion of affiliation with

NATIVE AMERICANISM.

Nativism. Even Scott, the Whig candidate for President in 1852, said *peccavi*. In the lull which followed the prostration of the Whigs a new form of the old movement was, however, starting into vigorous growth. This was Know-Nothingism.

The Know-Nothing Party.

I.

ORIGIN AND GROWTH.

THE Know-Nothing order was the outgrowth, in form and membership, of a number of nativist secret societies, which came into being during the years 1845-9. In Pennsylvania, the order of United American Mechanics, which restricted its membership to native-born Americans, had considerable strength. The order of Sons of America, organized about the year 1845, at Philadelphia, also acquired a large following, and even extended its branches to New York. Pennsylvania gave birth also to the American Prot-

estant Association, a secret benevolent
society composed of Protestant Irish.
This association also extended to New
York. In 1853 it had several thousand
members.

The Order of United Americans was
established in New York about the
year 1845, and it soon became the
strongest of the nativistic societies.
At the beginning of 1847, it had about
2,000 members, and in 1848 it had extended to Boston and organized itself at
points in New Jersey and Pennsylvania. Though ostensibly a social and
beneficial society, it now began to be
active in promoting, in a secret way,
certain political measures, and New
York politicians were not slow to de-
tect its influence.

Meanwhile, in the spring of 1850,
Charles B. Allen had organzied
the order of "the Star Spangled Banner," sometimes known as the
order of "the Sons of the Sires," its
purpose not being specifically social and
benevolent, like the other nativist secret
societies, but more definitely designed
to influence, by concerted action, local
elections.

Early in 1852, this new secret society

received a large increase of membership, drawn mostly from the Order of United Americans. It at once began to take a hand in politics. And this was the beginning of the Know-Nothing order.*

Both the Order of United Americans and the Know-Nothing order, otherwise known as the order of the Star Spangled Banner, then began a career of rapid expansion. In 1856, the Order of

---

*So far as primary sources of history are concerned, we have very little to aid us in tracing the course of the Know-Nothing movement. If even the records of so late a movement as the American Protective Association have been burned (as its founder, H. F. Bowers, informs me), what can we expect as to the records of a secret movement of fifty years ago? Scisco (Political Nativism in New York, p. 255), says: "The great Know-Nothing order has left hardly a trace of itself in the way of records." The records of the Know-Nothing grand council, after passing from one grand secretary to another, have disappeared. The private papers of James W. Barker, for many years the Know-Nothing leader, and of Erastus Brooks, a later leader, cannot be found, or are unavailable. Some of the records of the order of the United Americans were burned.

Contemporaneous manuals and defenses of the American party, like the volumes of Whitney, Carroll and Lee, seem to conceal more than they reveal.

United Americans had extended to sixteen states, and it had on its rolls several hundred thousand members. The order of the Star Spangled Banner, or the Know-Nothing order proper, had, meanwhile, far out-stripped the Order of United Americans. The name of Thomas R. Whitney is associated with the growth of the Order of United Americans. He was its grand sachem for the state of New York in the year 1846, and again in 1853. He was also the author of a book in defense of the Know-Nothing movement.

The more active political element of the Order of United Americans began to flock into the order of the Star Spangled Banner during the year 1853. The new order began to be active in seeking to control party caucusses and party conventions. Then, after the old parties made the nominations, the order of the Star Spangled Banner proceeded to elect its ticket from the Democratic and the Whig tickets.

November 10, 1853, The New York Tribune referred to the new secret influence in politics, which had been exerting itself for some months, as "the Know-Nothing order." The New York press explained, as the reason for the name, the fact that members of the order, when questioned, professed to "know nothing" about it.*

By the fall of 1853, the Know-Nothing order had organized branches in New Jersey, Pennsylvania, Maryland, Connecticut and Massachusetts, and had extended as far west as Ohio.

While Charles B. Allen was the founder, James W. Barker was the man most conspicuous in the up-building of the Know-Nothing order, especially in New York; and up to 1856 he was its official head in that state. Barker had been a dry goods merchant in New York in the years prior to 1851. He threw himself into the new nativist movement with all the zeal and energy that he possessed. We are told that

---

*Lee in his "History of the American Party," page 200 says: "Whether the American Associations are really secret associations or not is a question concerning which the writer pretends to know nothing." The new movement itself accepted in a certain way the "Know-Nothing" appellation. Thus we find one of its publications entitled "The Know-Nothing Calendar and True American Almanac for 1856," edited by W. S. Tisdale, Esq.; and also "The Wide-Awake Gift and Know-Nothing Token for (1855)," by 'One of 'Em.' "

in 1859 he left New York and again embarked in the dry goods business in the city of Pittsburg.

The Know-Nothing order was not a mutual aid or beneficial society, but its primary aim was political. It had the usual pass-words, grips and ritual of a secret society. There were three degrees with appropriate obligations and advantages.

Those inducted into the first degree do not appear to have been informed as to the name of the order. They were brought into "the august presence of Sam." Their oath recited, among other things, "that you will not vote or give your influence for any man for any office in the gift of the people, unless he be an American-born citizen, in favor of Americans ruling America, nor if he be a Roman Catholic." Members of the first degree were not eligible for office in the order, nor on its political tickets. Members of the second degree took an oath, one of the obligations of which recited "that if it may be done legally, you will, when elected or appointed to any official station conferring on you the power to do so,

54

remove all foreigners, aliens or Roman Catholics from office or place, and that you will, in no case, appoint such to any office or place in your gift; you do also promise and swear that this and all other obligations which you have previously taken in this order, shall ever be kept, through life, sacred and inviolate."

These extracts are from the ritual said to be revised by the national council held in Cincinnati on November 15, 1854. There were earlier publications of the oaths varying in their texts, but quite similar in their general antagonism to naturalized citizens and Catholics*

The third degree, as revised by the national council November, 1854, was the so-called "Union degree," pledging members to support the ties which bind together the states of the union and to oppose all men and measures adverse

---

*The constitution and ritual of the American party are published in full in N. W. Cluskey's "Political Text Book and Encyclopedia" (1858) pp. 55-68. Also in Cooper's "American Politics" (1882) p. 57. Scisco's account of the Know-Nothing degrees and ritual is drawn largely from the newspapers of the day.

to the union, and to vote for third or union degree members of the order in preference to all other candidates for political office.

The basis of the Know-Nothing organization was the ward or district council. In the large cities there was a superior council made up of delegates from the ward councils. The "grand council" was the state council made up of three delegates from each council of the order within the state. The national council, which was the supreme authority in the order, was made up of delegates from various states in which the order existed on a basis proportionate to the state membership.

The Know-Nothing order sought to keep from outsiders not only the identity of its membership, but even the fact of its existence. Its notices of meeting, or calls for concert of action were bits of paper cut in different shapes or varying in color for different purposes.

The leading circumstances and influences which contributed to the growth of the Know-Nothing movement may be briefly indicated as follows:

(1) Undoubtedly, the nativist sentiment, about which the whole movement swung, not only gave the party its form, but in a large degree was the cohesive influence which held together the principal element of its membership.

(2) The movement was launched after the overwhelming Whig defeat of 1852. That election seemed to many the end of all hope for the Whig party; the time for it and its friends to quit the political field. There ensued also a lessening of the ties of allegiance to party among the northern Democrats, due to the subserviency of Pierce's administration to the slavocracy. The thousands of voters cast adrift, so to speak, from their party affiliations, were easily attracted by the standards of the new movement. Had the Republican party been launched as early as 1853 or 1854, its sails might have been filled with the new breeze, but as it was not there, the Know-Nothing movement had the chance of the hour all to itself.

(3) The attraction of the secret society and the mystery of the movement

undoubtedly won to the Know-Nothing party thousands of Americans who had no special devotion to its more fanatical purpose.

(4) Its growth in the south and its absorption there of the Whig party, were altogether matters of political calculation. The southern Whigs thought that the sweep which the new party had won (1854-5) in the middle and New England states, promised a victory at the approaching presidential election in 1856. The southern Whigs thought they were getting on the loaded wagon. Except in Baltimore, Louisville and New Orleans, there was, south of Mason and Dixon's line, little chance for collision with foreign-born citizens, as few of them had settled there. Southern politicians, however, might reason themselves opposed to foreign immigration, inasmuch as confining itself almost entirely to the north, it swelled the congressional representation of the northern states.

(5) Another element drawn into the Know-Nothing party, especially the latter years of its existence, consisted of those who preferred to evade the slavery question, the "dough-faces," so-

called, in the political parlance of the times,—those who relied upon the constitution and who proclaimed their devotion to the union, vainly supposing that by taking such a stand they could postpone the irrepressible conflict on the slavery issue. The American party, virtually straddled the slavery question: and this attitude undoubtedly attracted to its ranks thousands of those who wished to take middle ground. In its last years, so far as it existed as a power in the politics of the country, it was not a middle state party, but a border state party.

II.

HIGH TIDE (1854-5).

IN his history of the Rise and Fall of the Slave Power (chapter 32), Henry Wilson, who had himself joined the Know-Nothing order, says: "In the year 1853, a secret order was organized by a few men in New York city. Its professed purpose was to check foreign influence, purify the ballot box and rebuke the effort to exclude the Bible from the public schools." Scisco, a more careful historian, at least in the matter of dates, (Political Nativism, p 97), reports:

"By May 1, 1853, there existed in New York state fifty-four scattered bodies, most of which were located in New York city or in the counties lying adjacent, where Nativistic sentiment had been fostered by the O. U. A. and other Nativistic societies. The spring elections of 1854 gave opportunities for the rural bodies to use their power, but nowhere does their presence seem to have attracted notice except in New York and Westchester counties."*

But local elections in the early months of 1854, in several adjoining states showed that the order was not

*Whitney, in his "Defence of the American Policy," (p. 284), says that state councils of the order of the United Americans were organized in New York, New Jersey, Maryland, Connecticut, Massachusetts, Pennsylvania and Ohio during the months April to December, 1853; in Washington, D. C., New Hampshire, Indiana, Rhode Island and Maine during the months January to April, 1854; in Illinois, Michigan, Iowa and Wisconsin from May to September, 1854. State councils were organized in the following southern states chiefly during the latter part of 1854: Alabama, Georgia, North Carolina, South Carolina, Kentucky, Missouri, Tennessee, Virginia, Delaware, Mississippi, Texas, Florida, Arkansas and Louisiana. In the fall of 1854 state councils were organized in California and Oregon. A state council was formed in Minnesota in May, 1855, and about the same time in New Mexico, Kansas and Nebraska. Thus, (says Whitney) , in about three years from the organization of the first council the order was organized in every state and territory in the Union, "numbering in its membership at least one and one half million legal voters."

only widely diffused, but so numerically strong, as to indicate that it had been organized for some time in these localities. There is some authority for the statement that was introduced in Baltimore in December, 1852. Salem (in January), Worcester and several other Massachusetts towns were carried by its silent influence in the spring election of 1854. At Philadelphia, it surprised the Democrats, (May, 1854), by electing the Whig candidate for Mayor, Conrad, by eight thousand plurality. Mayor Conrad proceeded openly to affiliate with the American party. About the same time Washington went under the Know-Nothing yoke and Baltimore followed.

In 1853-4 the Know-Nothing party acted largely upon the following formally adopted policy:

"Rule Nine: Whenever it shall be deemed necessary for the order to aid in the choice of men for public office through the suffrages of the people, it shall be the duty of each executive committee to call together the members of the Order in their district prior to the usual primary elections or nominations, and determine upon suitable candidates

of each party or either, as they may determine. It will be the duty of the
members to assemble at the times and
places of holding the primary meetings
of such party or parties, and there use
their influence in obtaining the nomination of the candidates they have selected. If the nominations are secured
and ratified our cause will triumph,
whichever party may be successful.
Should the members of the Order nominate or select candidates already in
the field, nominated by one party only,
it will be the duty of every brother to
sustain that selection independent of
any party consideration." (Scisco Political Nativism, p 80.)

In the congressional elections of 1854
—at which time the new power in politics became the sensation of the hour—-
this rule was quite generally followed.
The Know-Nothings—throughout the
north—supported Whig, Republicans
and anti-Nebraska Democratic candidates for congress, who were privately
pledged to so-called "American ideas."

When the congress thus elected met for
its first session in December, 1855, there
were over a hundred congressmen from
the north classified as Republicans;

they voted for the Republican candidate for speaker, N. P. Banks, but Horace Greeley, (writing at the time to Charles A. Dana,) said:

"The majority of the Banks men are now members of Know-Nothing councils, and some twenty or thirty of them actually believe in the swindle. Half the Massachusetts delegation, two-thirds that of Ohio, and nearly all that of Pennsylvania are Know-Nothings this day. We shall get them gradually detached." (Quoted in Rhodes History of the United States, Vol. II. p. 111.)

The manner in which the new power in politics set the tongue of the nation wagging over its entry into the arena was not through the silent influence it exerted in selecting congressmen, but by the showing it made with candidates of its own for governor in New York and Massachusetts. Its candidate for governor in New York (in the fall of 1854), was a man little known, and no open campaign work was done in his behalf, nor did any influential paper support him. Its candidate for governor in Massachusetts was a broken down Whig politician, whose appearance in the campaign was referred to by one of the leading Boston dailies as a joke.

To the surprise of everybody, it polled 122,000 votes for its candidate for governor of New York. Seymour, the Democratic candidate, had 156,495 votes, and Clarke, the Whig candidate, who was elected, had 156,804. In Massachusetts, Henry J. Gardner, the Know-Nothing candidate was elected governor by 50,000 majority, and the Know-Nothings elected both houses of the Legislature almost to a man. Delaware was also carried by the Know-Nothings.

These victories greatly accelerated the numerical growth of the order in the north and caused it to spread like wild fire through the south.

By March, 1855, J. W. Barker, the head of the order in New York, reported that there were nine hundred and sixty councils of the American party in his state alone. Its prospects were such that its success in the coming presidential election was seriously canvassed. The Worcester Evening Journal claimed that it would sweep the north and carry there more than enough electoral votes to secure the presidency. The New York Herald about the same time, (cited by Hambleton, History of the Political Campaign of Virginia in 1855, page 251), editorially declared that the American party would triumph in the coming presidential election if it could divest itself of its abolitionist handicap.

The Herald estimated the Know-Nothing votes at 1,375,000. Henry Wilson thinks they numbered not less than 1,250,000.

Viewing this episode in American politics, thirty years after, Bryce, the English historian (American Commonwealths II. p. 291), is moved to say:

"They [The Americans] are a changeful people. The Native American, or so-called Know-Nothing party, had, in two years from its foundation, become a tremendous force rising, and seeming likely for a time to carry its own presidential candidate. In three years more it was dead without a hope of revival."

But shrewd American political leaders, even while Know-Nothingism was at its high tide had forecasted its early disruption. Greeley's famous dictum:

"It [Know-Nothingism] would seem as devoid of the elements of persistence as an anti-cholera or anti-potato rot party" was written long prior to 1856.

Though the mortal hurts that the Know-Nothing movement received had been dealt in May and June, 1855, it still appeared to be ascendant in the fall elections of that year. It carried Massachusetts, New Hampshire, Rhode Island and Connecticut, electing the governors and legislatures in all these states and it elected the minor state officers voted for in the New York state election. It also elected its candidates for governor in Kentucky and California. It carried the legislature in Maryland and elected some minor candidates on the ticket which it put up in Texas. In Virginia, Alabama, Louisiana, Georgia, Mississippi and Texas it was beaten only by a close vote. The Democrats retained these states by majorities ranging from 2,000 to 10,000.

Meanwhile there occurred the signal defeat of the Know-Nothing ticket in the Virginia state election of May, 1855 and the split over the slavery issue in the Philadelphia convention of the

American party in June, 1855. These two events, together with the rise of the Republican party, presaged the rapid decline of the Know-Nothing movement.

Virginia was a debatable state—usually Democratic, but always so on a narrow margin. The state elections of 1855 were to determine whether the American party in absorbing the Whig party had strengthened or weakened the opposition to the Democratic party in the south. It was a very bitter struggle. The Democratic candidate for Governor, Henry A. Wise, made a vigorous denunciation of Know-Nothingism the feature of his campaign. He went from one end of the state to the other, delivering fifty speeches during the canvass. It was one of the record campaigns of the time. The attention of the whole country was drawn to this election. Great sums of money were wagered upon the result. Wise was elected by 10,-000 majority.

Commenting on the Virginia election, the New York Tribune of May 29, 1855, said that it "had rung the knell" of Know-Nothingism in the

South. It was reasoned that as a vote getter, the new party could not do much better in the slave states than the old Whig party had done.

Following this reverse came the split in the National Council of the Know-Nothing party which met at Philadelphia on June 5, 1855. The slavery issue had to be met in some way and a committee on resolutions had the subject up for three days discussion. Finally the majority of the committee recommended that Congress ought not to prohibit slavery in any territory and that it had no power to exclude any state from coming into the Union, because the state constitution recognized slavery. Delegates from thirteen free states brought in a minority report and another three days discussion followed, Henry Wilson leading the anti-slavery forces; but the Southern view triumphed by a vote of 80 to 59.*

Thereupon the delegates from Maine, New Hampshire, Vermont, Massachusetts, Connecticut, Rhode Island, Ohio,

*E. B. Bartlett, of Kentucky, superseded J. W. Barker of New York, as President of the order, although Barker, who was a candidate for re-election, trimmed to the southern view of the slavery issue.

Indiana, Michigan, Illinois, Iowa and Wisconsin left the convention.

In the ensuing elections the Know-Nothings at the south conducted their campaign on the slavery plánk adopted by the majority; but the Know-Nothing delegates from the free states issued an address repudiating that portion of the platform.

III.

DISTURBANCE AND ACRIMONY.

ONE of the internal troubles of the Catholic Church in the United States during the year subsequent to 1820, was the "trustee" system, whereby the lay trustees of many of the congregations assumed to a less or greater extent the authority to accept or reject the priests sent to minister over the congregation by the bishop, and to regulate the affairs of the parish in a manner that sometimes brought them into collision with the episcopal authority. Out of this conflict grew two incidents which gave the Know-Nothing movement a decided impetus.

The Pope sent Archbishop Bedini as papal nuncio to Brazil in 1853, and because of some troubles with church trustees in Buffalo and Philadelphia, Msgr. Bedini was requested by the

Pope to visit the United States on his way and endeavor to adjust these difficulties. He called on President Pierce at Washington bearing a letter, the intent of which was to give him standing as one of the diplomatic corps. At that time the United States had a minister accredited to the Pope, as temporal ruler of the Papal states, and there could be no objection, in international law, to the Pope accrediting a diplomatic representatives of his own to the United States. However, objection was interposed by the American state department to the reception of Msgr. Bedini as a diplomatic agent on the ground that he was not a layman.

There was then in the United States an ex-monk (a Barnabite) from Italy named Gavazzi, delivering about the country such lectures as a typical "ex-priest" is in the habit of presenting to the credulous American Protestant. Gavazzi had assailed Bedini, calling attention to his conduct as papal governor of Bologna during the troublous times of 1848, and his severity towards the revolutionists. The American press was inclined to assist the anti-Bedini

feeling aroused by Gavazzi; and un-
friendly crowds awaited the papal
nuncio's coming in various cities. At
Cincinnati, especially, there was a
threatening demonstration, a howling
mob of two thousand people moving
upon the house of the archbishop. The
militia were called out, and except for
this and the prompt action of local authorities, incendiarism and murder
would have resulted, for there were
leaders desirous of making an exam-
ple out of the incident by hanging
Msgr. Bedini. In some places, as in
Baltimore, where he was hanged in
effigy, he was obliged to conceal his
presence. He left the country without settling the disputes in question.

The other incident was a discussion
between Senator Brooks of the New
York Legislature and Bishop Hughes
(who signed himself "✝John, bishop
of the province of New York"license).
Brooks made some extravagant asser-
tions as to the value of Catholic church
property, incident to the discussion of
a bill pending in the legislature,
which sought to regulate the tenure
thereof. The measure advocated by
Senator Brooks was passed.

73

It provided that no title to real property could be conveyable or descendible by an ecclesiastic to his successor in office (Laws of 1855, Chapter 230). The intent of the measure, doubtless, was to compel Catholic bishops to divest themselves of the title to church property, and to vest the same in civil corporations. Because of so many difficulties with lay trustees, this plan was obnoxious to them. Subsequently, in the history of the Catholic Church, a policy in favor of placing all church property under protection of legal incorporation was, however, adopted. In the Third Plenary council of Baltimore this change was urged by the bishops. In 1863, a special act for the incorporation of Catholic church property was placed upon the New York statutes (ch. 45, Laws of 1863). At present, under the laws of several of the states, Catholic bishops are either authorized to act as corporations sole, for the purpose of holding real estate, or the New York system for the incorporation of the local churches with the bishop, the vicar-general, the pastor and two laymen as the board of directors, is followed.

The riotous events which signalized the visit of Archbishop Bedini continued during the ensuing year, largely excited by anti-Popery street preachers. The "Angel Gabriel," an eccentric Scotch anti-Popery speaker, was at work in New England in 1854, and numerous anti-Catholic disturbances resulted. A Know-Nothing mob made an attack upon the Irish quarter in Chelsea. In June, 1854, the Catholic chapel at Coburg was burned. In the early part of July, the Dorchester Catholic chapel was blown up by the Know-Nothings. A little Catholic church at Bath, in Maine, was burned to the ground. A mob paraded the streets of Manchester, N. H., tore the American flag from the priest's house and wrecked the interior of the Catholic church. At Ellsworth, Me., Father Bapst, the Catholic priest, was taken from his dwelling and tarred and feathered.

These events excited Catholic apprehension in all parts of the country, and the business of guarding the Catholic churches from incendiarism and mob violence became a serious purpose with them. At Providence, R. I., in the same year, a Know-Nothing mob, led by a notorious criminal, attacked the Convent of Mercy, but the damage was slight, as the Catholics rallied for the protection of the institution. August 7 and 8, St. Louis was the scene of a riot precipitated by the Know-Nothings, which resulted in ten deaths and the destruction of a number of houses of Catholics. The election riots at Baltimore, and "Bloody Monday" at Louisville will be elsewhere noted. At Washington a Know-Nothing mob forced its way into a shed near the Washington monument and captured a block of marble, taken from the temple of Concord at Rome, which had been sent by the Pope as a tribute to be used in the monument then being erected to Washington. This papal gift was thrown into the Potomac.

One of the earliest outcroppings of Know-Nothingism in New York transpired over the case of a street preacher named Daniel Parsons, who had been indulging in bitter anti-Popery speeches on Sundays about the wharves and docks. The authorities placed him under arrest. Immediately there was a movement of protest from the Know-Nothings. A great meeting was called in the City Hall park. Thousands were present, and James W. Barker, the Know-Nothing leader, presided. Parsons was released and went on with his work.

On the first Sunday of June, 1854, an anti-Catholic preacher was escorted through Brooklyn by a Know-Nothing mob of 5,000. This no-Popery demonstration collided with an Irish mob, and a free fight ensued. On the following Sunday the disturbance was renewed.

During the spring of 1854, a young man named Patten, organized in New York a nativist secret society for younger men. They were known as the Order of the American Star, and sometimes as The Wide-Awakes, from their rallying cry. This organization attended to all street disturbances on behalf of the order. Their white felt "wide-awake" hats were recognized as the insignia of their belligerant purpose.

In Massachusetts, one of the first acts of the Know-Nothing governor, Gardner, in 1855, was to disband all militia companies in which foreigners predominated. These included six Irish-American companies, the Columbus, Webster and Shields National guards of Boston, Jackson guards of Lowell, Union guards of Lawrence and Jackson guards of Worcester.

All through the years 1853 and 1854 the anti-Catholic propaganda was fed by a remarkable crop of sensational sermons, pamphlets and novels, and the republication of numerous works of evangelical bigotry dating from the epoch of Catholic emancipation (1829).

In many places throughout the north the children of Irish parentage attending the common schools, were subjected during these years to various kinds of petty persecution. On the school grounds they were hooted as "Paddies," text-books were utilized to disparage their religion, but the most usual form of annoyance had reference to Bible reading. Numerous cases of this kind went into the courts; that of Donohue vs. Richards, which transpired at Ellsworth, Me., in 1854, where a Catholic pupil was subjected to corporal punishment for declining to read the Protestant scriptures, being the most notable.

It is to the credit of our courts that the narrow-minded position of the Maine Supreme bench in this case did not receive the approval, subsequently, of any court of final resort. Later in the fifties, a hundred Catholic children of the Elliot school in Boston were expelled because they refused in a body to participate in Protestant prayers and Bible reading. In 1859, Principal Cooke of one of the Boston schools, severely punished Thomas J. Whall, a Catholic pupil, who had declined to recite the Ten Commandments according to the King James version. The case went into one of the local courts, but without redress to the plaintiff.

In 1853 and 1854 the Know-Nothings used secret machinery to interfere with and disturb the political meetings of their opponents of other parties. George W. Julian tells us: "If a meeting was called to oppose and denounce its schemes, it was drowned in the Know-Nothing flood which, at the appointed time, completely overwhelmed the helpless minority. This happened in my own county and town, where thousands of men, including many of my own Free Soil brethren, assembled as an organized mob to suppress the freedom of speech, and succeeded by brute force in taking possession of every building in which their opponents could meet, and silencing them by savage yells." (Julian's "Political Recollections," 142.)

Charles Reemlin, a prominent foreign-born Republican of Ohio, in his "Review of American Politics" (page 214), says that "in Know-Nothing times there was a tacit exception from anti-foreign objuration in favor of Scotch and English Protestants.* * The foreign-born Presbyterians were in fact, a sort of back-stair members of Know-Nothing lodges."

After 1848, there came to the United States among the increasing German immigration, a large number of men imbued with the revolutionary spirit of the time. This German element was bitterly hostile to church influence; and also inclined to believe that the American system of government could be reformed. The German Social Democratic association of Richmond outlined a program of reforms, and the Free Germans of Louisville adopted a similar platform calling for the abolition of the presidency and the Senate, the abrogation of Sunday laws, of oaths taken upon the Bible, etc. In Maryland, Kentucky and Tennessee these German programs were widely used to excite Know-Nothing hostility to immigration. The German element also was more adverse to the institution of slavery than were the other foreign elements. Most of the German papers of the country showed a tendency to support the new Republican party. The keen politicians of the south perceived this. "While in the north the crusade was carried on mainly against the Irish," says Von Holst (VI. 188), "the south was chiefly concerned in insuring the harmlessness of the wicked Germans." Mobbing of German newspapers and Turner halls in some of the cities in the border states were incidents noted in the newspapers towards the eve of the civil war.

IV.

DEMOCRATIC AND REPUB-
LICAN ATTITUDES.

MANY anti-Nebraska Democrats
went into Know-Nothing lodges
in 1854. The secret movement undoubtedly promised to shape Democratic nominations as well as Whig and
Republican nominations in that year.
Congressman Carruthers (Dem.) of
Missouri, admitted (Feb. 28, 1856), in
a letter to his constituents that he had
joined the order:

"I went twice (and but twice), into
their [the Know Nothing] councils. I
'saw Sam.' It took two visits to see
him all over. I made them. I saw enough
and determined never to look on his
face again."

N. P. Banks stated in the House
that he secured his first election (in

1852) to Congress through a combination of Democrats and Know-Nothings.

Cutts says that Douglas told him: "The [Know Nothing]party struck terror everywhere among the Democrats, and threatened to gain absolute posession of the government. I tried to get the Democrats in caucus to denounce it, but they refused, and were afraid. General Cass said to me that I had enough to contend with, and could not carry on my shoulders this new element. I was the first Democrat to make a speech against it. I did so at Independence hall, Philadelphia," [July 4, 1854]. (A Brief Treatise upon Constitutional and Party Questions . .* * * as I received it orally from * * * St. A. Douglas p. 121.)

Douglas and Wise leading the way, other Democratic politicians joined in the denunciation of Know Nothingism, and purged the party of the taint. In April, 1855, at Murpheesboro, Tenn., Gov. Andrew Johnson, (Dem)., delivered a strong speech against it, and in May, 1855, Alexander Stephens of Georgia published a letter denouncing it.

The Democratic members of Congress, which convened December, 1855, unlike their predecessors in the previous Congress, knew where they ought to stand on the Know-Nothing issue. Fresh from the mandate of the people, they took occasion, in their first party caucus, to declare themselves against Know-Nothingism.

The Democratic platform upon which Buchanan was elected President in 1856, was unequivocal in this matter. It recited:

"That the liberal principles sanctioned in the Constitution which makes ours the land of liberty and the asylum of the oppressed of every nation have been cardinal principles of the Democratic faith; and every attempt to abridge the privilege of becoming citizens and owning soil among us ought to be resented." And:

"Hence a political crusade in the nineteenth century and in the United States of America against Catholics and foreign born, is neither justified by the past history nor future prospects of the country, nor in unison with the spirit of toleration and enlightened freedom which peculiarly distinguishes the American system of popular government."

The formation of the "Republican" party was first suggested at a meeting of anti-slavery men convened March, 1854, at Ripon, Wisconsin, and this was followed in July, 1854, by Republican movements in Michigan and Vermont. But the Republican movement did not at once take hold throughout the country. The old Whig party refused to disband in New York and Massachusetts, and the Know Nothings placed all obstacles possible in the way of the new party. The demand of the northern anti-slavery sentiment for a political organization gradually found expression, however, after the middle of 1854,—in some states, as in Indiana where it chose the title "People's party"—under differing names and auspices, but with a general similarity of aims and purposes everywhere.

The earnest anti-slavery men who founded the Republican party were generally outspoken antagonists of Know Nothingism; not entirely, of course, because they disliked its intolerance, but because they revolted at its truce with the slavocracy. Wade, Giddings and Julian were among those who early denounced the Know Nothings. In a speech in the Senate on the Homestead bill, William H. Seward took occasion (February, 1855) to remark:

"It is sufficient for me to say that, in my judgment, everything is un-American which makes a distinction, of whatever kind, in this country, between the native born American and him whose lot is directed to be cast here by an overruling Providence, and who renounces his allegiance to a foreign land and swears fealty to the country which adopts him."

And Henry Ward Beecher wrote in The Independent (January, 18, 1855: "By years of persistent labor, the conscience and honor of multitudes of the north had been aroused. They began to see and value the real principles fundamental to American institutions. Under the shallow pretense that Know Nothing lodges would, by and by, become the champions of liberty, as now they are of the Protestant faith, thousands have been inveigled into these catacombs of freedom. One might as well study optics in the pyramids of Egypt, or the subterranean tombs of Rome, as liberty in secret conclaves controlled by hoary knaves versed in political intrigue, who can hardly enough express their surprise and delight to see honest men going into a wide-spread system of secret caucuses. Honest men in such places have the peculiar advantage that flies have in a spider's web—the privilege of losing their legs, of buzzing without flying, and being eaten up at leisure by big-bellied spiders."

Greeley in The New York Tribune, and Dr. Bailey in The National Era, were strongly anti-Know-Nothing. All the extreme abolitionists and their organ, The Liberator, were adverse on principle to the proscriptive movement.

The first state convention of the Republican party in Illinois, (Bloomington, March, 1856), inserted in its platform a resolution denouncing the Know Nothings. Abraham Lincoln was present as a delegate. When the anti-slavery men of New York (in the latter part of 1855), finally came together to launch the Republican party, the platform reported by Horace Greeley and adopted by the convention, strongly condemned the methods and the doctrines of the Know Nothings.

February 22, 1856, a national convention of the Republicans met at Pittsburg, and when Charles Reemlin and other speakers vigorously denounced Know Nothingism as a mischievous side issue, they were loudly applauded. At the subsequent national convention of the Republican party in June at Philadelphia, the platform upon which Fremont was nominated declared * * "believing that the spirit of our institions as well as the institutions of our country guarantees liberty of conscience and equality of rights among citizens we oppose all proscriptive legislation affecting their security."

This view was substantially reiterated in the platform of the Chicago national convention of the Republican party in 1860, section 14, reciting that "the Republican party is opposed to any changes in our naturalization laws" and favors "protection to the rights of all classes of citizens, whether native or naturalized."

Former Know Nothings sat in these conventions and heard the principles of their recent affiliation denounced, but they made no objection. Either their eyes had been opened, or the evil training of surreptitious politics deprived them of the courage of their convictions.

The Republican party absorbed thousands of those who left the Know Nothing lodges and its politicians tempered their methods in the years 1857-9, in such wise as to catch the fragments of the disrupting American party.

Chas. A. Dana, for instance, wrote Sept. 1, 1859:

"The Americans hold the balance of power in both [N. J. and N. Y.] Their party is in the act of final dissolution. Shall we let the fragments fall into with the arms of the Locofocos." (Pike p. 444).

There was an effective warning, however, against truckling in this process to any Know-Nothing policy. Thus Lincoln, in 1859, wrote a public letter against "the waning fallacy of Know-Nothingism," (see Nicholay and Hay's Biography, II., 181), with special reference to the Know-Nothing naturalization idea.

Horace Greeley ("Recollections" p. 290), expresses this opinion, which as a forecast, undoubtedly governed the managers of the Republican party after 1856:

"The fact that almost every Know Nothing was at heart a Whig or a Democrat, a champion or an opponent of slavery and felt a stronger, deeper interest in other issues than in those which affiliated him with the 'Order', rendered its disruption and abandonment not a question of years, but of months."

It is not the less true or creditable, however, that the initial expressions of the Republican party and of its leaders were unequivocally against the Know-Nothing movement.

V.

KNOW-NOTHINGISM AND ITS ISSUES.

THE national convention of the American party at Philadelphia, in June, 1855, made the following statement of the distinctive principles of Know-Nothingism:

"A radical revision and modification of the laws regulating immigration, and the settlement of immigrants, offering the honest immigrant, who from love of liberty or hatred of oppression, seeks an asylum in the United States, a friendly reception and protection, but unqualifiedly condemning the transmission to our shores or felons and paupers.

"The essential modfication of the naturalization laws. The repeal by the legislatures of the respective states of all state laws allowing foreigners not naturalized, to vote. The repeal, without retrospective operation, of all acts of Congress making grants of land to unnaturalized foreigners, and allowing them to vote in the territories.

"Resistance to the aggressive policy and corrupting tendencies of the Roman Catholic Church in our country; by the advancement to all political stations, executive, legislative, judicial or diplomatic—of those only who do not hold civil allegiance, directly or indirectly, to any foreign power, whether civil or ecclesiastical, and who are Americans by birth, education and training, thus fulfilling the maxim, 'Americans only shall govern America.'

"And inasmuch as Christianity, by the constitutions of nearly all the states; by the decisions of most eminent judicial authorities, and by the consent of the people of America, is considered an element of our political system, and the Holy Bible is at once the source of Christianity and the depository and fountain of all civil and religious freedom, we oppose every attempt to exclude it from the schools thus established in the states."

The platform of the American party in 1856, upon which Fillmore was nominated, covered the ground of the preceding platform as follows:

"Americans must rule America, and to this end native-born citizens should be selected for all state and municipal offices, or government employment, in preference to all others.

"No person should be selected for political station (whether of native or foreign birth), who recognizes any allegiance or obligation of any description to any foreign prince, potentate or power, or who refuses to recognize the federal and state constitutions (each within its sphere), as paramount to all other laws as issues of political action.

"A change in the laws of naturalization, making a continued residence of twenty-one years, of all not hereinbefore provided for, an indispensable requisite for citizenship hereafter, and excluding all paupers and persons convicted of crime, from landing upon our shores, but no interference with the vested rights of foreigners."

On the slavery issue, the sincere men in the '50's—the men who knew what they wanted and who were earnest about it—were the Republicans of the north, who opposed the further extension of slavery, no matter what the consequences; and on the other side, the Democrats of the south, who wanted the sectional equilibrium maintained, slavery extended equally with the spread of freedom, a new slave state for every new free state, and if this could not be, the south would secede.

Between these parties stood many who temporized, or compromised, or trimmed; and the Know-Nothings were conspicuously of this class. They took the position that their issues,—naturalization, immigration and papal aggression were the important and vital issues,—and that the slavery issue must, for the sake of the union and sectional harmony, be left where legislation up to the year 1855 found it.

But as northern opinion continued to turn against the political dominance of the south, provoked by the demands which the slavocray made, and exacted from the Democratic party (embodied in such events as the Kansas-Nebraska bill, the Fugitive Slave law and the Dred Scott decision), a large element of the northern Know-Nothings, whether from policy or conviction, found that they could no longer straddle the slavery issue. Numbers of these went into the Republican party; numbers of them adhered to the American party under protest as to its position on the slavery issue.

At the national convention of the Know-Nothing order at Philadelphia in June, 1855, there were two reports on the slavery question from the committee on resolutions. The majority, consisting of fourteen members from the southern states and the representatives from New York and Minnesota, declared that Congress ought not to prohibit slavery in the District of Columbia or in any territory, that it had no power to exclude any state from admission to the union because that state, by its constitution, allowed slavery. The minority, consisting of the representatives from thirteen free states, proposed that the Missouri compromise should be re-enacted, and that no part of the Kansas-Nebraska territory should come into the union as a slave state. After a protracted debate, the majority report, as has been noted, was adopted (80 to 59). The minority protested, but the northern wing of the party nevertheless, continued to act with the southern wing. Their anti-slavery sentiment was a matter of policy rather than of conviction. This was illustrated at the subsequent national gathering of the party at Philadelphia in February, 1856, when the platform being under consideration, Mr. Sheets of Indiana, pleaded for a more ambiguous statement on the slavery issue for the sake of the northern Know-Nothings; "he was willing to accept the Washington platform; for if there was anything in it, it was so covered up with verbiage that a president would be elected before the people found out what it was all about (tumultuous laughter)."*

Southern opinion, both Democratic and Whig, in so far as it was concerned about the slavery question, regarded the Know-Nothing movement complacently, as a diversion in political tactics, and as such calculated to impede the

---

*In the course of debate, Parson Brownlow of Tennessee, declared he could "take five men of his delegation and lick the Ohio delegation out of the hall."

growth of the anti-slavery sentiment in the north. Julian's view on the matter is, of course, far-fetched, but it indicates correctly the practical advantage the southerner might look for:

"Its [the American party's] birth, simultaneously with the repeal of the Missouri compromise, was not an accident, as any one could see who had studied the tactics of the slave-holders. It was a well-timed scheme to divide the people of the free states upon trifles and side issues, while the south remained a unit in defense of its great interest. It was the cunning attempt to balk and divert the indignation aroused by the repeal of the Missouri restriction, which else would spend its force upon the aggression of slavery; for by thus kindling the Protestant jealousy of our people against the Pope, and enlisting them in a crusade against the foreigner, the south could all the more successfully push forward its schemes." (Political Recollections. 1840 to 1872, p. 141.)

Southern opinion rather welcomed a northern movement to shut out European immigration. Immigration had largely increased the preponderance of

the north in the popular branch of
Congress, and given that section its
army of western settlers now peopling
the territories for freedom. Governor
Smith of Virginia said in a speech,
reported in The New York Tribune,
March 14, 1855: "The origin of the
Know-Nothings is a struggle for bread
—a frightful and angry question at
the north. At the south it is a political question of high importance. The
north has fifty-five more representatives
than the south already. The natural
increase of the south is one-third greater than that of the north, because there
are greater checks on population there;
but the artificial element of foreignism
brings 500,000 who settle annually in
the free states, with instincts against
slavery, making fifty representatives in
ten years to swell the opposition to
the south. To stop this enormous dis-
proportion, what is our policy? What
is the frightful prospect before us?
The effect of Know-Nothingism is to
turn back the tide of immigration, and
our highest duty to the south is to discourage immigration. I deprecate it
as a great calamity."

A slaveholder of the period put the

matter in this way: "The mistake with us has been that it was not made felony to bring in an Irishman when it was made piracy to bring in an African." (Draper's American Conflict, I., 446.)

VI.

SOLVENT INFLUENCES AND
DISCUSSION.

AFTER 1854 the Know-Nothing movement was subjected to the solvent influences of public opinion. The press of the country sought to drag it into the open. Its extension into the south was accompanied by a loss of secrecy. The American party there adopted the open methods of the Whig party which it absorbed. "It does the south no small honor," says Von Holst, (V. p. 191), "that there the party had to agree to give up its secrecy and its oaths as it had already been forced there to make concessions in regard to the Catholics."

Col J. W. Forney, in an address on "Religious Intolerance and Political Proscription" delivered at Lancaster,

Pa., 24th Sept. 1855, p. 22, tells us:

"To such extent has public indignation been excited against the profane and familiar resort to extra judicial oaths, and the invariable appeal to force and fraud at the ballot-boxes, that in portions of the Union it [the American party] has deliberately discarded alike its secrecy and its obligations. This has been the case in Alabama, Georgia, Louisiana and South Carolina."

The secrecy of the order was practically done for throughout the whole country after the American party launched itself in national politics. When in June, 1855, the Know-Nothing national convention assembled at Philadelphia, its sessions were fully reported in the New York papers whose representatives were present at the gathering. State councils of the Know-Nothing order there were empowered to dispense with the secret character of the movement. The platform declared:

"That each state council shall have authority to amend their several constitutions so as to abolish the several degrees, and institute a pledge of honor instead of other obligations for fellowship and admission into the party. A free and open discussion of all the political principles embraced in our platform."

This option was speedily availed of. The Massachusetts Know-Nothings, for instance, on August 7, 1855, abolished secrecy, including the oaths. (Life of Bowles, 140).

One consequence of the loss of secrecy and the turning on of the light of public discussion was the attempted disavowal and abatement of the intolerant program of the order and the desuetude of its obligations against the Catholics and foreigners. This happened quite generally in the south and more particularly in the states of Louisiana and Missouri; but also in California.

L. M. Kennett of Missouri, himself a Know-Nothing congressman said of the party in his state: "All secrecy is there discarded and religious tests ignored." (Cluskey, The Political Text book p, 299). Congressman Barry of Mississippi, speaking December, 1854, in the House of Representatives said: "In Louisiana Catholics are allowed to join the order because that denomination is too numerous there to be assailed openly." Congressman Eustis of Louisiana, elected as a Know-Nothing, delivered a speech Jan. 6, 1856, in the House of Representatives in which he entirely repudiated the anti-Catholic policy of his party and passed to a eulogy of Catholic citizenship.*

In Illinois the Know-Nothing order split into two factions, "the Sams" insisting upon an anti-Catholic program and "the Jonathans" proposing not to antagonize Catholics who owed no civil allegiance as distinguished from spiritual allegiance to the Pope. The Jonathans triumphed.

But even in the south, in the course of political discussion, when the American party was forced to defend its intolerant program, its advocates borrowed the narrow and inflamatory arguments of their northern brethren; though they preferred to avoid this line of discussion and many of them succeeded in doing so.

---

*Two sets of delegates appeared from Louisiana at the Philadelphia Know-Nothing convention in 1856. And among the members of one it was ascertained that there were Catholics.

There were, too, numerous splits in the order, growing out of personal jealousies and contests for power.

When the Grand Council of New York, in October 1854, put up a candidate for governor it was claimed that this was done without consulting the subordinate councils. The Grand Council then complained that its candidates were defeated at the polls because a large number of Know-Nothings had not voted for them. An attempt was made to discipline the bolters and this widened the breach. The Brooklyn Council objected to such coercion by resolutions which described the action of the Grand Council as "equalled only by the Holy Inquisition of Spain."

Allen, the father of the order, was impelled to organize a seceding movement; and the "Know-Somethings," the "North Americans," the "Mountain Sweets" and other designations, which are found in the newspapers after 1854, indicate the progress of such disintegration.

While the Nativist and anti-Catholic movement was inevitable and would have occurred even if the Irish and Catholic element had been on their best behavior and had given no provocation whatever, it is interesting to note how far the Catholics held themselves blameable. Dr. Brownson, the eminent Catholic publicist of that day, in his Quarterly Review (Works, vol. 10, page 317), said of the Irish element: "The great majority of them are quiet, modest and peaceful and loyal citizens adorning religion by their faith and piety and enriching the country by their successful trade or their productive industry. But it cannot be denied that hanging loosely on to their skirts is a miserable rabble unlike anything which the country has ever known of native growth—a noisy, drinking and brawling rabble, who have after all a great deal of influence with their countrymen, who are usually taken to represent the whole Irish Catholic body, and who actually do compromise it to an extent much greater than good Catholics, attentive to their own business, commonly suspect or can easily be made to believe."

As for the proper policy for Catholics to pursue in the matter, Dr. Brownson wrote as follows. (Quoted in the Life of O. A. Brownson, Vol, 2, Page 539):

"We Catholics are in a small minority and the sentiment of the country is strongly anti-Catholic. Every measure that we oppose as hostile to us, the country will favor and adopt and every measure we support as favorable to our interests, it will reject. I am sorry that it is so, but so it is; and I think that in regard to matters which depend on popular votes, and in which we are interested as Catholics, the more quiet we keep the better it will be for us."

This advice was not followed by Dr. Brownson's co-religionists. They everywhere met their "dark lantern" antagonist openly and with vigor. They fought it through their press and they fought it through the political party to which most of them belonged; for undoubtedly it was due to the large Catholic and Irish element in the Democratic party that Douglas and other Democratic leaders purged their party of the Know-Nothing element and made it not neutral, but openly hostile to the Know-Nothing policy.

No matter how good the behavior of the Catholic and Irish element might have been, the old charge of the evangelical church party in England and

106

America that the citizenship of the Catholic is a matter of divided allegiance would have formed the main charge of the Know-Nothing movement. The Catholics denied the charge. Brownson wrote:

"In acknowledging the equal rights of all religions the American system acknowledges that the state has no authority in spirituals and therefore in religious matters has no claim to the obedience or allegiance of any of its subjects or citizens. Hence as the Pope has only authority over Catholics in the spiritual order, no obedience he can exact of them, or which they owe him, can ever conflict with any obedience which the state with us even claims as its due." (Brownson's Works Vol. 18. page 345.)

But he also trenched upon what, in this country at least, will always be a purely academic issue: whether in case of conflict between the temporal and spiritual order, which must yield? "The temporal of course" answered Brownson. This branch of the discussion was quite a needless one to enter on, especially too as it subjected Dr. Brownson and his co-religionists to a

107

great deal of misrepresentation and Brownson personally, to the attack of most of the Catholic and Irish-American papers of the country, which regarded him as an extremist in his view of this matter. John Mitchell, then editing the Irish Citizen of New York, assailed Brownson as follows:

"This I say has been your work Doctor Orestes; hence has come whatever of bitterness and ferocity that is to be found in the Native-American party; this outrageous caricature of Catholicity, held up to America by you (after you had tired of all the other religions) has been the principal spring, and is the only excuse for the furious anti-Irish spirit which is now raging."

Not only Brownson's Quarterly Review, but other Catholic papers were widely misquoted in Know-Nothing publications; and in this discussion their language was garbled and not a few sheer fabrications were set afloat. It is to be noted that so respectable a historian as Von Holst in the fifth volume of his Constitutional History, taking quotations from Brownson's Review, second hand as he finds them in Know-Nothing publications, is misled as to the Catholic attitude in the discussions referred to. An alleged quotation from a St. Louis publication called The Shepherd of the Valley, which has done service in anti-Catholic literature for nearly half a century and the garbled nature of which has been frequently exposed, is accepted by Von Holst in his array of evidence as to Catholic opinion.

But these misquotations of Catholic authorities were merely incidents in the discussion. They were not necessary to bolster up the time honored Anglo-Saxon and Evangelical aspersion of the integrity Catholic citizenship, an aspersion as old as the age of Queen Elizabeth and responsible for the persecuting statutes of her time; an aspersion too, which though diminishing in force from generation to generation is, nevertheless, liable to recur in years to come and during future flurries of intolerance.

VII.

THE CAMPAIGN OF 1856.

ON Washington's birthday, Feb. 22, 1856, the American party met at Philadelphia to nominate a presidential ticket. The selection of a candidate for president was easily made. Fillmore led with 71 votes on the first ballot, a scattering opposition giving George Law 27 votes, Garret Davis 13, R. F. Stockton 8, Judge McLean 7, Sam Houston 6, John Bell 5, Kenneth Raynor 2, Erastus Brooks 2, John M. Clayton of Delaware 1 and L. D. Campbell of Ohio 1. A. J. Donnelson of Tennessee was nominated for vice-president. The American ticket was endorsed, a few months later, by a national convention of the old line Whigs at Baltimore.

The Republican party assembled in Philadelphia in June, and nominated

John C. Fremont for president. On the informal ballot, 359 votes were cast for Fremont and 196 for McLean.

Around the candidacy of McLean, then a judge of the supreme court of the United States, there gathered something of interest in the history of Know-Nothingism. He had been a cabinet officer under Monroe and John Quincy Adams, and he was appointed to the supreme bench by Andrew Jackson. The secession of a number of northern delegates from the American convention at Philadelphia in February, had entered into the calculation of the Republicans who sought to attach those delegates to their cause. It was generally understood that the anti-slavery Americans favored McLean. The German element of the country, then largely affiliating with the Republican party, took alarm. A great majority of their papers, of which there were then a hundred in the country, clamored for Fremont, probably through fear of McLean's supposed nativist tendencies. Delegates from the doubtful states, and many conservative Republicans, were inclined to favor McLean as the more available candidate. They thought

111

that he would make a better run against Buchanan in Pennsylvania, which was then a pivotal state. On that account Stevens, Lincoln, Washburn and many others, advised his nomination. Fremont's nomination, on the formal ballot was, however, almost unanimous.

The Know-Nothings, who seceded from the Philadelphia American convention, ultimately endorsed Fremont, though they first nominated Banks, who declined. Fremont's nomination, however, was not acceptable to a certain other element of the "North Americans." They further seceded and nominated Stockton of New Jersey for president.

In the ensuing campaign the noise and hurrah throughout the north were decidedly with the Republicans. They gave the country a livelier season of electioneering than any it had seen since 1840; indeed, old politicians seem to agree that '56 was even more rousing than the Tippecanoe and Tyler campaign. It was increasingly apparent that the American party had no chance of victory. In Pennsylvania, which was then an October pivotal state, the

Republican and Know-Nothing managers came together to patch up a plan to wrest that state from Buchanan by arranging a union state ticket. The plan failed. Pennsylvania was carried in October by the Democrats against the combined votes of the other parties; and again for the national ticket in November. Buchanan received 174 electoral votes, to 114 for Fremont and 8 for Fillmore. This campaign ended the American party as a national organization.

The distribution of the popular vote received by Fillmore, the candidate of the American party, was as follows:

FREE STATES.		SLAVE STATES.	
Maine 3,335		Virginia.. 60,310	
New Hampshire .422		No. Carolina. ..36,886	
Vermont...... 545		So. Carolina	
Massachusetts. 19,626		Georgia.. 42,228	
Connecticut 1,675		Alabama.. 28,552	
Rhode Island.... 2,615		Florida.. 4,833	
		Mississippi 24,195	
	28,218	Louisiana.. 20,709	
New York 124,604		Texas.. 15,639	
*New Jersey... 24,115		Arkansas.. 10,787	
*Pennsylvania. 82,175		Missouri.. 48,524	
		Tennessee.. .. 66,178	
	230,894	Kentucky.. ... 67,416	
Ohio.. 28,126		Delaware... 6,175	
Michigan.. 1,660		Maryland.. 47,460	
*Indiana.. 22,386			
*Illinois.... 37,444		Total.... 479,882	
Wisconsin.. 579			
Iowa.. 9,180			
*California.. ...36,165			
	135,540		
Total.... 394,652			

The free states (5) marked with a

113

star, and all the slave states except Maryland, were carried by Buchanan, giving him 174 electoral votes. Fremont carried 11 of the 16 free states, giving him 114 electoral votes, and Fillmore carried Maryland alone, giving him 8 electoral votes. The American party cut but little figure in this election in the New England states and in the northwest. In Illinois it cast about sixteen per cent. of the total vote, and in Ohio and Indiana less than eight per cent. In California it cast one-third of the total vote, and in New York, New Jersey and Pennsylvania, less than one-fourth. The north cast less than one-seventh of its total vote for the Know-Nothing presidential ticket, and the south about three-sevenths of its total vote: the north something less than fifteen per cent, and the south something over forty per cent. More than half, or 480,000 of the 874,-000 votes given Fillmore, came from that portion of the United States south of Mason and Dixon's line, and but 394,652 from the free states.

The popular vote of the free states was thus divided as between the candidates: Of a total of 2,961,009 northern voters, 1,340,070 voted for Fremont, the Republican candidate, 1,226,287 voted for Buchanan, the Democratic candidate, and 394,652 voted for Fillmore, the American candidate. In the total southern vote of 1,092,995, 611,-879 voted for Buchanan, 479,882 for Fillmore and only 1,094 voted for Fremont.

The Know-Nothing vote in the south, however, is not so significant as bearing upon the question of religious and nativist intolerance as the vote in the north. It did not signify much beyond the gathering of the Whig opposition under a new banner, but held together by the same Whig principles, associations and leaders. In the north, however, the Know-Nothing vote of 1856, wherever it appeared, usually signified a much larger degree of existing religious and racial prejudice.

The vote of New England showed that this state of feeling had been swept away almost entirely by the deeper interest felt in the slavery issue, but the old nativist root feeling in New York, New Jersey and Pennsylvania still persisted, and possibly held a fifth of the voters of those states in willing bondage; and to some extent the same intolerant feeling was influential in Ohio, Indiana and Illinois, where, perhaps from five to ten per cent of the voters still thought the Pope a more vital issue than slavery.

The Whig vote of the south in 1852 had been 367,000. The American party of 1856, with 480,000 votes in the south, virtually absorbed the strength and natural increase of the Whigs. It came closest to carrying the old-time Whig states of Kentucky, Tennessee and Louisiana, which, since 1836, had generally gone for the Whig presidential candidate. Maryland, which Fillmore carried, was also naturally a Whig state. It had given its electoral vote to the Whig candidate for president at every election since 1836, that of 1852 alone excepted.

VIII.

KNOW-NOTHINGISM IN CONGRESS.

ALTHOUGH the thirty-third congress, elected at the time of the presidential election in 1852, and convening for its first session in December, 1853, and for its second session in December, 1854, was overwhelmingly Democratic (Democrats, 159; Whigs, 71; Free Soilers, 4), there was not wanting a suspicion that a number of its members, many of them Whigs, but some Democrats, had been inducted into the Know-Nothing order, or were under obligations to the new movement for support at the polls. In February, 1855, Congressman Witte of Pennsylvania, introduced a resolution in the House condemning secret political societies and their proscriptive purposes; and he moved a suspension of the rules so that the resolution could be discussed; at the same time, declaring that the vote on the suspension of the rules would be regarded as a test vote. The House refused to suspend the rules,—ayes 103, noes 78—the necessary two-thirds vote in the affirmative not being obtained. Had all the Democrats voted for the suspension of the rules, that motion might have easily carried. Those Democrats who voted in the negative explained their course by stating that a prolonged discussion upon the resolution would interfere with the transaction of a mass of business which had been accumulating in the committeees of the House.

The thirty-fourth congress, elected at the fall elections of 1854, was divided, in so far as a classification was possible, as follows: In the Senate, 42 Democrats, 15 Republicans and 5 Know-Nothings. In the House, 83 Democrats, 108 Republicans (70 of whom were members of Know-Nothing councils), and 43 out-and-out Know-Nothings. The Know-Nothings held the balance of power. There then ensued a prolonged contest for the speakership,

118

one of the most remarkable episodes of the kind in our congressional annals. Both Democrats and Republicans seem to have bid for the American vote. Men of Know-Nothing affiliation were prominent among the candidates. On the first ballot Humphrey Marshall of Louisville, Ky., one of the Know-Nothing leaders of the border states, received 30 out of the 225 votes cast. N. P. Banks of Massachusetts, first a Democrat, then a Know-Nothing, but now a Republican, received 21 votes. H. M. Fuller, leader of the conservative Know-Nothings, received 17 votes. L. D. Campbell of Ohio, anti-slavery Know-Nothing, 53 votes. After two months of continuous balloting, N. P. Banks, the Republican candidate, was finally elected speaker by a plurality vote.

At the presidential election of 1856, the Know-Nothings met with reverses. The thirty-fifth congress, which was then elected, began its session in December, 1857, and was constituted as follows: In the Senate 39 Democrats, 20 Republicans and 5 Know-Nothings; in the house 131 Democrats, 92 Republicans and 14 Know-Nothings. Orr

119

(Dem.) was elected speaker. He was unequivocably against the Know-Nothings.

The thirty-sixth congress, elected in the fall of 1858, met for its first session in December, 1859, and was constituted as follows: In the Senate, 38 Democrats, 26 Republicans and 2 Know-Nothings; in the House, 101 Democrats, 113 Republicans (four of whom were Know-Nothings), and 23 Know-Nothings (openly classed as such). By this time the Know-Nothing party, especially so far as it appeared in Congress, was a border-state party. Its two senators were from the states of Kentucky and Maryland. Of its twenty-three congressmen, five came from Kentucky, seven from Tennessee, three from Maryland, four from North Carolina, two from Georgia and one each from Louisiana and Virginia. Pennington (Rep.) was chosen speaker, receiving 117 votes to 85 for his Democratic opponent.

As the American party was never anything but a mere minority or third party, in Congress, it naturally had little influence upon national legislation. "Humphrey Marshall, a Kentucky

Know-Nothing, said that he found no American party in Washington; that the engrossing subject was the negro." (Rhodes History of the United States —II., 117).

"Know-Nothingism," says Von Holst (V., 129), "disappeared without having accomplished the least thing against immigrants, adopted citizens or Catholic.

IX.

LAST YEARS.

AFTER 1856, the disintegration of the Know-Nothing order was rapid. It had carried Maryland and Rhode Island in the state election of 1856, and in these states and in Kentucky and Tennessee it continued to retain some political power; but the question in practical politics with respect to it was: "Where will the fragments fall?" In New York the Democrats were able to pick up some strength by absorbing a portion of the Know-Nothing element. We find, for instance, Erastus Brooks becoming, in the course of years, a Democrat in good standing, so that in 1868 he went as a delegate to the convention of the Democratic party which put Seymour in nomination for the presidency. Millard Fillmore, in 1864, openly supported McClellan for the presidency. In Ohio, some years later, we find Campbell, one of the leaders of the Know-Nothing party in that state, enrolled with the Democratic party. The larger element of the party in the northern states drifted into the anti-slavery movement represented by the Republican party.

In the speakership contest of 1859-60, the border-state Americans held the balance of power. The Democrats, at one period of the contest, sought to win the speakership by combining upon Smith, an American congressman from North Carolina. He received 112 votes January 27, 1860,—within three votes of an election. When Pennington, the Republican candidate, was finally elected speaker, February 1, 1860, he received 117 votes, among them the votes of two Americans, Briggs of New York and Henry Winter Davis of Maryland.

Another episode of interest in the absorption of the Know-Nothing following occurred in the Chicago Republican convention of 1860. Two-thirds of the delegates to that convention are said to have favored the nomination of William H. Seward. Several influences combined in depriving Seward of

123

what was almost within his grasp. The feeling that he might prove too radical a candidate to be available, and the criticism to which he was exposed in his own state on various grounds had their bearing; but in the view of many historians the question of his availability as presidential candidate in Pennsylvania and Indiana also figured. In these states the Republican party was depending for its success upon the complete absorption of the Know-Nothing following, and Seward's outspoken denunciation of the Know-Nothing movement, and his entire career, since 1840, as towards the nativist movement, were considered factors that would count against him. As a consequence, the Republican candidates for governor in those states influenced their delegations against Seward.

The Constitutional Union party, which nominated Bell and Everett as candidates in 1860, was made up chiefly of the jetsam and flotsam of the American party not yet absorbed by the other parties. Bell was a member of the American party, and Everett had supported Fillmore in 1856. The Constitutional Union movement was organized by such border and southern state Americans as Crittenden of Kentucky and Houston of Texas. Fillmore's total vote in 1866 was 874,000; Bell's in 1860, 646,000; but while Bell maintained Fillmore's strength in the slave states, where he received 516,000 as compared with Fillmore's 480,000 in 1856, in the free states Bell received only 130,000 as compared with Fillmore's 394,000 in 1856.

X.

LOCAL SKETCHES.

IT remains to make special mention of Know-Nothing activity in certain localities where it worked itself out more fully and typically as an influence in city and state politics.

The career of the Know-Nothing party in Maryland is noteworthy by reason of the fact that this was the only state carried by the American party in the presidential election of 1856; that Know-Nothingism persisted here as a political force longer than in any other locality, the Know-Nothings holding the reins of government in Baltimore from the fall of 1854 to the fall of 1860; and also for the election riots and disorders which Know-Nothingism perpetrated in Baltimore.

Twice, (in 1855 and in 1857), the

Know-Nothings carried the state Legislature. In the latter year they elected a candidate for governor by reason of a large fraudulent vote cast in Baltimore.

The picturesque, and at the same time the repulsive, feature of the reign of Know-Nothingism in Baltimore was the roughing of elections. In October, 1854, the Know-Nothing candidate was elected mayor of Baltimore by a majority of two thousand. In 1856 Thomas Swann, a former president of the Baltimore & Ohio railroad, was the Know-Nothing candidate for mayor of Baltimore, and he was elected by a majority of fifteen hundred. After this the Know-Nothings ruled Baltimore and Maryland with a high hand. They carried Baltimore for their candidate for governor in 1857 by over nine thousand majority, and at the municipal election of 1858 they re-elected Swann mayor by a majority of 19,154 out of a total vote of 24,003. They again carried the city in the fall of 1859 by a majority of 12,000 for their state ticket. The Legislature chosen this year was Democratic, and the growing, but heretofore impotent popular disapproval of the way the elections were run in Baltimore, now succeeded in enacting a practical remedy. The control of the Baltimore police was taken out of the hands of the local officials and vested in a commission designated by the Legislature. Under the improved police system, disorder at the polls was prevented, and a fair election made possible, and so in the municipal election of 1860, the Know-Nothings were overwhelmingly defeated. The reform party elected its candidate for mayor by over 8,-000 majority. Thus, after six years of riotous control, the Know-Nothings were driven forever from the citadel of their power.*

Disorders at local elections were frequent in New York and Philadelphia, as well as in Balitmore, in the years 1840 to 1860. Baltimore and its Know-Nothings, however, carried such excesses to the limit. Among the Know-Nothing clubs of the city

*For a full an interesting account of the Baltimore American party, see L. F. Schneckebier's "History of the Know-Nothing Party in Maryland" (Johns Hopkins University Studies, series 17, No. 4-5.)

which figured in these disorders, were
the Tigers, the Black Snakes, the
Rip Raps, the Blood Tubs and more
especially the Plug Uglies. There were
clubs on the Democratic side such as
the Bloody Eights, the Bloats and the
Buttenders, no less euphonious in name
and disorderly in conduct; but after
1856 the Democrats virtually laid
down, leaving the Know-Nothings the
monopoly of disorder and ruffianism.

In the municipal election of October,
1856, the Plug Uglies flocked down towards the Eighth ward to attack the
Democratic partisans, and in a riot,
lasting several hours, four men were
killed and over fifty wounded. In the
following month, at the presidential
election, this rioting was renewed, the
Know-Nothing clubs wheeling a cannon
through the streets; ten men were killed and over 250 wounded. In the elections of the succeeding years, the only
ward in which the Democrats could
vote without danger was the Eighth
ward, where the Irish element was
strong. In most other wards only
Know-Nothings, who gave the proper
signal, could get to the polls, all other
citizens being pushed aside or intim-

idated. In some instances, bodies of
voters to the number of a hundred or
more were cooped up in cellars until
the election was over. The governor
of Maryland sought, in 1857, to induce
the Know-Nothing mayor of Baltimore
to take effective steps against election
disorder, but his efforts were in vain.
In the following years the shoe maker's
awl became a favorite Know-Nothing
weapon of intimidation. Plug Ugly
clubs paraded the streets carrying
transparencies showing the figure of a
man running, with another, in pursuit
sticking an awl into him.

An interesting episode in the history of the state of Massachusetts was
its famous Know-Nothing Legislature,
which convened in the first week of the
year 1855. The upper house was solidly Know-Nothing. The lower house
was also Know-Nothing, with the exception of one Democrat, one Whig and
one Free Soiler. One of the opposition papers suggested as a text for the
customary election sermon to be preach-
ed before this Legislature, "For we are
but of yesterday and know nothing."
(Job 8, 9). In this Legislature there

were about half as many farmers as the average in previous state Legislatures, but there were four times as many clergymen. Twenty-four ministers sat in the upper and lower houses.

The most notable event of the session was the appointment of a committee to inspect the nunneries, the so-called "smelling committee." This committee, which was under the lead of one Hiss, a "Grand Worthy Instructor" of a Know-Nothing council, became a junketing affair, and carried along with it a number of invited guests. Its members lived at the best hotels and drank expensive wines at the cost of the state. The hotel expenses of a notorious woman were included among its many vouchers.

A writer in The Boston Advertiser of that period thus describes the committees' visit to a convent:

"The gentlemen—we presume we must call members of the Legislature by this name—roamed over the whole house from attic to cellar. No part of the house was enough protected by respect for the common courtesies of civilized life to be spared the examination. The ladies' dresses hanging in their

131

wardrobes were tossed over. The party invaded the chapel and showed their respect—as Protestants, we presume—for the One God whom all Christians worship, by talking loudly with their hats on; while the ladies shrank in terror at the desecration of a spot which they hallowed."

Under pressure of public clamor, the Legislature began to investigate its investigating committee, and three successive committees were necessary for the task. Hiss was finally expelled from the House by the votes, so he claimed, of men who had enjoyed the hospitality of the committee.

The following lines were written by some satirist of the time:

"One after one the honored Bay-leaves
 fade,
And ancient glories wither in the shade;
The solon's of the state, at duty's call,
Have hissed a loving member from the
 hall.
Take courage, Joseph, in thy great ado;
The world has hissed the Legislature, too."

Further investigations followed, bringing to light a series of petty stealings. George W. Haines, in his interesting sketch of this Know-Nothing Legislature (The American Historical Asscn. vol. 8, part 1, page 187) states that the notion was widespread among its members that cheating the government was only a venial offense. It was, says Congdon (Recollections of a Journalist, 146), "the most illy- assorted legislative body that ever met in this country."

The only distinctively nativist measure passed by the Legislature was a proposed amendment to the constitution restricting office-holding to native-born Americans, and requiring twenty-one years residence for naturalization. The proposed amendment, however, was never submitted to popular vote, nor did it receive the endorsement of the succeeding Legislature. Another measure, in which we have the prototype of such legislation as the Bennett law of Wisconsin and the Edward's law of Illinois (A. D. 1890), was introduced by one Johnson, who claimed that he sought a seat in the Legislature for that express purpose. This measure proposed to extend public supervision over all private schools, to the end that the state should see that its requirements in the matter of education were met by the course of study and text-books, and, presumably, the teachers employed in such private and church schools. Johnson's measure, however, was not pressed by his colleagues.

New York city, though the cradle of nativism, and the headquarters of the controlling Know-Nothing clique, was not captured, politically, by the American party, although strenuous efforts were put forth in that direction. In the local election of 1854, James W. Barker appeared as the Know-Nothing candidate for mayor. The factions of the Democratic party united on Fernando Wood as their candidate, and the Whigs nominated John J. Herrick. Both Wood and Herrick were at that time members of the Know-Nothing party. Wood was elected by a narrow plurality: the Know-Nothings claimed that Barker had been counted out. He received 18,547 votes. Wood was re-elected mayor at the city election in the fall of 1856 over the Know-Nothing candidate, Isaac O. Barker, a cousin of James W. Barker. Wood's plurality was about 9,000. In the local elections subsequent to 1856, the Know-Nothings did not depend on their own strength, but sought combinations.

134

Their vote dwindled from 8,500 in 1857, to a little over 4,000 in 1859. After 1856 the Republican party had become the real competitor against the Democracy in New York city, and the Know-Nothing party sank to a position of a third party. By the beginning of 1860 it had disappeared from New York city as a party organization.

In the municipal election of May, 1854, Conrad, the Whig candidate, was elected mayor of Philadelphia, receiving about 29,500 votes to 21,100 cast for Vaux, Democrat. The election was won by the Know-Nothing councils quietly determining to support the candidacy of Conrad. Subsequently, Mayor-elect Conrad took the position that all policemen should be of American birth, thus indicating that he was in sympathy with the Know-Nothing movement, although not elected as the nominee of that party. In the election of the following year the Know-Nothing party was successful in electing its candidates to all minor city offices voted upon; but in the municipal elections of May, 1856, the Democrats returned to power in Philadelphia, electing their candidate, Vaux, for mayor, by several thousand majority. In 1858, and again in 1860, the candidates of the opposing parties, adopting the name of "the People's party," triumphed over the Democrats in Philadelphia's municipal elections.

The nativist sentiment was always strong in the city of Boston. Thomas Aspinwall Davis, nominated by the native American party, was mayor of Boston in 1845, but the wave of Nativism soon subsided. The following year the Whigs regained political control of Boston. In 1854 the Native-American or Know-Nothing party elected Dr. Jerome Crownshield Smith mayor of Boston. He showed himself extremely fertile in making suggestions. In Winsor's History of Boston, (III. page 259) we read the "he (Smith) was never taken quite seriously as a chief magistrate." In the municipal election of December, 1855, the nominee of the Citizen's movement was elected over the Know-Nothing candidate by 2,000 majority. Boston was satisfied with one year of Know-Nothing rule.

In Louisville, Ky., the Know-Nothing movement was signalized in August 1855, by an election riot, the occasion being referred to as "Bloody Monday" in the annals of that city. Shaler in his History of Kentucky, (page 219), tells us that the disorder was occasioned by "roughs of the Native-American party attacking the Catholic people." Twenty-two persons were killed, two-thirds of whom were residents of the Irish quarter, and sixteen houses burned. In this election, which was for state officers, Moorhead, Know-Nothing candidate for Governor of Kentucky was elected, receiving 68,816 votes to 65,413 for Clarke the Democratic candidate.

"In Alabama the new party made some effort before 1855, and in the local conflict at Mobile, the Catholic property near that city was burned by American partisans" (Du Bose, Life of Yancey, p. 291). The Democratic mayor of Mobile, Jones M. Withers, affiliated in 1854 with the American party; but subsequently threw it over and ran again as a Democrat for mayor of Mobile and was re-elected.

The Know-Nothing movement appeared in a less pronounced form in many other cities besides New York, Boston, Philadelphia, Baltimore and Louisville. It was manifest in the local politics of Cincinnati. In Detroit in the municipal elections of 1855 a Know-Nothing candidate for mayor received 2,000 votes to 2,700 for the Democratic candidate and in San Francisco the Know-Nothings in the fall elections of 1855 polled 1,500 votes out of a total of 12,000.

XI.

PERSONNEL.

HENRY WILSON tells us (ch. 32,
Rise and Fall of the Slave Power),
that hundreds of those who joined the
Know-Nothing movement cared little
for its avowed principles, but were ea-
ger to possess and use its machinery.
"I did not dream," says George W.
Julian (Political Recollections p. 143),
"that in less than two years the men
composing this mob would be found
denying their membership in this secret order, or confessing it with
shame."

Edward Everett Hale says, "it was
distinctly a Philistine movement, so
far as its leaders went." As for the
rank and file, they were not anywhere
the better element of the native-born
population. A writer in The New
England Magazine (n. s. Vol. 15, p.

82), made a careful study of the roster of membership at Worcester, Mass., in 1854. He finds that a large percentage, in signing the rolls, misspelled the names of the streets upon which they lived; that there were few professional men among them, and that where they were tax-payers, they averaged far below the per capita of the community at large.

Thousands went into the new movement unthinkingly, but for the novelty of the thing, and without understanding its character. The case of Ulysses S. Grant is an illustration. He tells us in his "Memoirs" (Vol. 1, p. 169): "Most of my neighbors had known me as an officer in the army with Whig proclivities. They had been on the same side, and on the death of their party many had become Know-Nothings or members of the American party. There was a lodge near me [he then resided on a farm in the vicinity of St. Louis], and I was invited to join it. I accepted the invitation; was initiated and attended a meeting just one week later; and never went to another afterwards. * *
But all secret oath-bound societies are

dangerous to any nation. * * No political society can, or ought, to exist where one of its corner stones is opposition to freedom of thought, or the right of worshiping God 'according to the dictates of one's own conscience.' " Subsequently, Grant voted (1856) for James Buchanan, the Democratic candidate for president.

Undoubtedly, thousands of the southern Whigs went into the new American party as unconsciously, so to speak, as did Ulysses S. Grant in 1854. It would probably be incorrect to impute bigotry to many of those public men from the south, once representing the Whig party, but subsequently absorbed, and going with the mass of their constituents, into the Know-Nothing ranks. John J. Crittenden of Kentucky, John Bell of Tennessee, both members of the United States Senate, were classed with the American party. Crittenden had been for forty years in public life, a member of the cabinet and rich in the honors of the Whig party. Bell, spoken of as "the generous Bell," had also served in the cabinet of a Whig president. These two union-loving men found themselves stranded as political orphans in the last years of the American party, with whose more proscriptive principles it is fair, as well as charitable, to assume they had no real sympathy. Senator Adams of Mississippi was another Know-Nothing United States senator.

Anthony Kennedy of Maryland, was elected United States senator by the Know-Nothing Legislature of that state. Sam Houston, hero of the notable struggle of the Texas republic against Mexico, and who was United States senator from Texas from 1853-59, was affiliated with the American party, and undoubtedly leaned towards some of its principles. In 1854 he was questioned by Senator Mallory, on the floor of the Senate, as to whether he approved of the Know-Nothing doctrine that Roman Catholics should be ineligible for office. He replied that he would not vote for such a law, and could not approve of it. Houston received a few votes for president in the Democratic national convention of 1852, in the Know-Nothing convention of 1856 and in the Union Constitutional convention of 1860. He supported Fillmore in 1856. Fillmore's associate on the presidential ticket in 1856 was Donnelson of Tennessee, a nephew of Andrew Jackson. Donnelson had joined the Know-Nothing order with other Whig politicians of his state in 1853. Henry Winter Davis of Baltimore was member of Congress, first as a Whig in 1854 and subsequently as a Know-Nothing in 1856-58. Here he was the orator of the new party in all controversies ("the Rupert of debate"). He was undoubtedly smirched with some of the bigotry, and expressed not a few of the rabid sentiments of the movement. This may have been due to his habit of epigram as well as to his desire to please the Know-Nothing clubs of Baltimore. His Know-Nothing constituents censured him for helping to elect Pennington speaker of the House in 1860. He was again in Congress during the civil war as a Republican.

Among other "southern Americans," as they came to be called, were Kenneth Raynor of North Carolina, a strong unionist advocate; he, it was, who formulated the third, or union degree, of the order; Garrett Davis of Kentucky, Humphrey Marshall of Louisville, the

143

latter the acknowledged leader of the
border-state Know-Nothings, ex-Congressman Botts of Richmond, who was
mentioned for the presidential nomination in 1856, Call of Florida, Zollicoffer
of Tennessee, and Bartlett of Kentucky, who sought the vice-presidential
nomination in 1856.

In the presidential campaign of 1856,
the Know-Nothings taunted the Republicans with the charge that Fremont was a Catholic, and the Republicans retorted that Fillmore, the Know-Nothing candidate, was not a Know-Nothing; but although he had begun
political life as an anti-Mason, Fillmore, in his lust for the presidency,
had consented to be made a third degree Know-Nothing at Buffalo in 1855.
His public expressions were, however,
free from religious intolerance. Erastus Brooks, whom the Know-Nothings
nominated as governor of New York
in 1856, but who failed of election,
was prominent in the public eye on account of his discussion with Bishop
Hughes over Catholic Church property and its tenure.

Henry Gardner, elected governor of
Massachusetts by the American party

in 1854, and again in 1855, H. M. Fuller, leader of the conservative Know-Nothings of Pennsylvania, L. D. Campbell of Ohio, leader of the anti-slavery Know-Nothings, Governor Johnson of Pennsylvania, were other public men identified with the Know-Nothing movement. N. P. Banks, who succeeded Gardner as governor of Massachusetts, was elected to Congress in 1852, as he afterwards admitted, by a union of the Democrats and Know-Nothings. "In the spring or summer of 1854, Gen. Banks asked me whether I intended to join the Know-Nothings. I said no; that I had left politics, and that I intended to practice law. He said in reply: 'I am in politics and I must go on.'" (Boutwell's Sixty Years in Public Affairs, I., 238.) Banks was chosen speaker of the House after a prolonged contest, in February, 1856. Thereafter he affiliated with the Republicans. He became a general in the civil war, and returned to Congress after its close, serving in the lower house from 1865-74, and again in 1888.

Henry Wilson, afterwards vice-president of the United States from 1872-

76, after being black-balled by one Know-Nothing lodge, succeeded in obtaining admission to another. The Know-Nothing Legislature of Massachusetts elected him United States senator in 1855. He led the bolt of the free state delegates from the Know-Nothing convention at Philadelphia in the same year. After that he cast his lot with the Republican party. He is said to have regretted his early connection with the Know-Nothing movement. Congdon (Recollections of a Journalist, 146), says: "When he was running for the vice-presidency, and Catholic votes were desirable, if he did not himself deny the fact [that he had joined the Know-Nothings], he suffered others to deny it."

Another picturesque figure in this movement was George Law of New York city. Law was the son of a north of Ireland immigrant. He began life as a hod carrier, just as Wilson began life as a day laborer. By the year 1850, however, Law was a wealthy contractor, and a liberal patron of the nativist movement. His ambition was to be the presidential candidate of the American party in 1856, and he had

146

the support of a number of journals and a large personal following, perhaps held together by his financial largesses. In the presidential convention of 1856, however, Law received but twenty-seven votes out of a total of over two hundred; after which we hear little more of him. He died in 1881.

Richard W. Thompson of Indiana, who was afterwards secretary of the navy in the cabinet of President Hayes, was a Know-Nothing in 1856. George W. Julian, in his Political Recollections (p. 155), referring to the campaign of 1856, says: "Richard W. Thompson, then the professed champion of Fillmore, but in reality the stipendiary of the Democrats, denounced the Republicans as abolitionists." Thompson was evidently a Know-Nothing from conviction, judging by his "Footprints of the Jesuits," and other publications which came from his pen during the period 1872-95.

Four Know-Nothing governors were prominent in the Philadelphia convention of the party, June, 1855: Governors Gardner of Massachusetts, Fletcher of Vermont, Johnson of Pennsylvania and Brown of Tennessee.

Whitney (Defence of the American Party, p. 303), says:

"The question has often been asked: 'Why cannot an American paper be sustained?' The answer is plain. Every attempt to establish one, until recently, has been made odious through the Romish and partisan presses of the country." Americans feared to subscribe for such a paper, "lest they should share in the general obloquy, or suffer in their business and private relations." "An advertisement in them was regarded as a dangerous experiment."

But the Know-Nothing movement was not without a number of weekly exponents and at Worcester, Mass., it established a daily organ. At Louisville, the brilliant George D. Prentiss lent his pen to the proscriptive movement; and his paper was held largely responsible for the murders and incendiarism of Bloody Monday in that city.

XII.

AFTERWARDS.

MOST of those who continued to adhere to the American party during the latter years of its activity, voted, in 1860, for Bell and Everett, candidates of the Union party for president and vice-president. Bell had been a senator from Tennessee (1853-9) outspoken in favoring the nativist restrictions upon naturalization. The personal following of Erastus Brooks in the state of New York, made up largely of the more consistent Know-Nothings, were especially pronounced for the Bell and Everett ticket.

This was the end of the American party, however, as an organized influence. The Order of United Americans, which had grown and declined with the growth and decline of the Know-Nothing movement, maintained a feeble existence up to 1866, although according to its last grand sachem, Charles E. Gildersleeve, the active membership in New York city in January, 1863, was " so small, it could have met in one room." There were attempts to reorganize the movement after the close of the war. The old head of the Know-Nothing movement, James W. Barker, launched a new organization, called the Order of American Shield, which afterwards took the name of the Order of the American Union. It aimed to become a political influence, and established branches in sixteen states. But its life was feeble, and by the year 1880 it had everywhere died out. Some of the veteran members of the Know-Nothing society organized a social club in New York city in 1877, reviving for their club name the old title of "Washington Chapter, O. U. A."

The various hereditary patriotic societies, the organization of which was suggested by the recurrence of the centennial anniversary of Revolutionary events, appear to be entirely free from the nativist and anti-Catholic bias.

Among these orders are the Sons of the American Revolution, organized in 1875, the Daughters of the American Revolution, organized in 1892, the Sons of the War of 1812, the Sons of the Colonial Wars, the Colonial Dames, etc.

The "United Order of American Mechanics," organized in 1845, and having today a membership, variously reported as from 40,C0 to 60,000; the "Junior Order of American Mechanics," organized in 1853, and established in over thirty states, at present with a membership of about 100,000, and the "Patriotic Order of Sons of America," established in 1847, with a membership of about 50,000, are survivals of the nativist movement. Their membership is restricted to native-born Americans, and they adopt several of the old Know-Nothing planks in their platforms. They are probably everywhere anti-Catholic in their political activity. The bulk of the membership of these organizations is found in the middle states. The Knights of Malta, established in 1889, with a membership which has varied up to 25,000, is a beneficial organization, with general purposes similar to those of the Junior Order of United American Mechanics, but more distinctly Protestant in its constitution.

Another organization, pronouncedly anti-Catholic in its activity, is the "National League for the Protection of American Institutions," organized in New York in 1889, with John Jay as president, and Rev. James M. King as secretary. Its objects were to establish "constitutional and legislative safeguards for the American public school system," and to prevent the appropriation of public funds to sectarian or denominational institutions. It outlined a proposed "sixteenth amendment" to the constitution of the United States along these lines; and it secured the endorsement of a number of the leading American denominations for its proposition, but the idea failed to receive the required approval of Congress. The National League made itself conspicuously active in securing the confirmation by the Senate of Governor Morgan and Rev. Dr. Dorchester, whom President Harrison had nominated at the head of the Indian bureau. This was done with the express understanding that these appointees would discourage further appropriations to the Catholic Indian schools. In New York it opposed the freedom of worship bill, and although the measure was finally enacted, the League succeeded in blocking its passage for a number of years. This measure extended the benefits of the constitution, respecting freedom of conscience, to the inmates of the state reformatory and penal institutions. The league also opposed the building of the Catholic chapel at West Point. The chapel was subsequently built by an enabling act of Congress. In its efforts to amend several of the state constitutions in the direction of prohibiting the appropriation of public funds to sectarian institutions, Rev. James M. King, in his work, "Facing the Twentieth Century," (page 530) tells us that the National League met defeat in the state of Maine through the efforts of the Protestant institutions, which feared that a judicial interpretation of the word "sectarian," would cut off certain appropriations of public funds, which they were accustomed to receive.

THE KNOW-NOTHING PARTY.

There were many episodes, between the close of the civil war and the rise of the "new Know-Nothingism," symbolized in the A. P. A., which bore a relation to the Know-Nothing movement of the past, and which evidenced the persistence of the sentiment upon which that movement was builded.*

The Culturkampf, in Germany, after the close of the Franco-Prussian war (1872-6), had its echoes in the recrudescence of anti-papal sentiment in the United States. There were not wanting many pulpit divines, even some public men, like Richard W. Thompson, afterwards secretary of the navy under President Hayes, who believed that the Culturkampf should be adapted to conditions here, and vigorously pushed.

*A riot involving sectarian antipathies occurred at New York, July 12, 1871. It grew out of an attack made upon the Orangemen, who on July 12, 1870, celebrated the anniversary of the battle of the Boyne. They advertised their intention of organizing a notable parade July 12, 1871. On the other hand the Hibernian element threatened to prevent this parade. The protection of the state and city authorities was sought against this Irish menace. When the day came, 100 Orangemen paraded the streets guarded by five militia regiments. Near the

THE KNOW-NOTHING PARTY.

In the '70's, the Catholic parochial school movement of the United States received a definite and more systematic organization. The latent Know-Nothing spirit caught eagerly, as a signal for aggressive discussion, at some paragraphs in a Des Moines speech of President Grant, wherein he urged the necessity of keeping church and state absolutely separate, and preventing the division of the school fund. The pencil of the cartoonist, Thomas Nast, in these years, was devoted in Harper's Weekly to embittering public sentiment against the Catholic Church on the school question.

In the presidential election of 1876, we find the following notice taken at this issue in the platforms of the Republican and Democratic parties: Section 7 of the Republican platform recognizes "the public school system of the several states as the bulwark of the

corner of Eighth avenue and Twenty-fourth street, an Irish tenement district, the parade was assailed with stones and some shots were fired. The militia met this attack by a volley which killed fifty-one of the assailants and bystanders; three of the militia men were killed. Public opinion in New York sustained the authorities in their action.

American republic." The platform
further recommends an amendment to
the constitution prohibiting the appropriation of public funds to sectarian
schools or institutions. The Democratic platform refers to "the false issue
with which they [the Republican party]
would enkindle sectarian strife with
respect to the public schools," which
should be maintained "without prejudice to any class, sect or creed." The
Republican platform of 1880 substantially reiterates the plank of 1876.
The Democratic platform of 1880 re-
cites that common schools have been
fostered and protected by that party.

In the presidential election of 1880,
most of the New York papers, Democratic as well as Republican, condemned the nomination by the Democrats
of William R. Grace as mayor of New
York. It was the first time that a
Catholic had been nominated for that
office, and the school question, and papal allegiance, and the impolicy of
weighing down the Democratic National ticket with such a handicap, were
vigorously dilated upon. Grace was
elected, but he ran many thousands behind the vote New York city gave

General Hancock, the Democratic candidate for president. In the last days of the campaign of 1884, James G. Blaine, the Republican candidate for president, was given a reception by nearly a thousand Protestant ministers, at the Fifth Avenue Hotel, New York. Their spokesman, Rev. Dr. Burchard, in a fervent address, alluded to the Democratic party as one whose antecedents were "Rum, Romanism and Rebellion." Blaine saw the impolicy of the remark at the time, and his managers sought to have all note of it suppressed in the newspapers. Democratic politicians got hold of it, and worked it with such good effect, in recalling the drift of "the Irish vote" to the Republican standard, that in the close state of New York it made a difference of a few thousand votes against Blaine. These votes, nevertheless, deprived him of the electoral vote of New York, and, as a consequence, lost him the presidency.

A Boston school issue in 1886, furnishes a striking evidence of the easily inflammable anti-Catholic sentiment of that community. It arose over a very small matter—a foot-note in Swinton's General History, then in use in the Boston public schools. This foot-note referred to "the sale of indulgences" by the Catholic Church, as a cause of the Protestant reformation. Members of the Boston school board who were Catholics, succeeded in convincing the publishers that their book should be gotten out without this foot-note. Immediately, there was a bitter public controversy on the subject of indulgences, and the question came up in the election of the retiring school board with such effect that a board satisfactory to the ultra-Protestant view of this historical matter was elected. Afterwards Professor George Adams, of the department of history of Yale university, in a text-book of European History (p. 302), took a view of the question (undoubtedly clarified by this discussion), which indicated a conviction that the Catholics of Boston were rather justified in their contention.

An "American party" showed itself, briefly, in the state politics of California in 1886. Frank Pixley, publisher of The Argonaut, a weekly literary journal, anti-Catholic in its views, but of much literary merit, seems to have led this movement. It endorsed Swift, the Republican candidate for governor, but he repudiated its endorsement with an open and manly assertion of the doctrines of the constitution. The Democratic candidate, Bartlett, was elected governor by a few hundred plurality. The American party mouthpiece asserted that, if Swift had kept silent, he would have won. The American party disappeared from the politics of California in the ensuing year.